NEWTON PAGE

NEWTON PAGE

THOMAS MUN
THE COMPLETE WORKS:
ECONOMICS AND TRADE

A Discourse of Trade from England unto the East Indies
(1621)

England's Treasure by Foreign Trade
(1664)

by

Thomas Mun

NEWTON PAGE

NEWTON PAGE

www.newtonpage.com

Thomas Mun
The Complete Works:
Economics and Trade

A Discourse of Trade from England unto the East Indies

(1621)

England's Treasure by Forgeign Trade

(1664)

by

Thomas Mun

Front cover image taken from
'The Foreign Trade' by Abraham van Strij

1 3 5 7 9 10 8 6 4 2

ISBN 978-1-934619-11-7

Printed in the United States of America
Set in Adobe Garamond Pro

CONTENTS

ENGLAND'S TREASURE BY FOREIGN TRADE (1664)

NOTE ON THE TEXT

Since the two works contained in this collection were first published almost four hundred years ago, conventions of spelling, grammar, punctuation, expression, word-truncation, vocabulary and general notation have each undergone considerable modernization. In addition, the relatively crude assembly practices of seventeenth-century book and pamphlet production have been gradually replaced by the radically more exacting standards of modern publishing, which demand both uniformity of typesetting and editorial consistency. As a consequence of those changes, the modern reader is used to a much simpler, cleaner and polished product than those available in the 1600s.

However, notwithstanding the usual expectations of the modern reader, and in full appreciation that the original texts are not as easy on the modern eye as they would have been on an early eighteenth-century equivalent, the temptation to edit them to conform with modern writing and publishing conventions has been resisted. That approach has been taken because to do anything other than retain the original form of Mun's works would be to detract from their inelegant and colorful original character.

There are three minor technical exceptions to the above. First, certain archaic letter forms, which fell out of favor in the late eighteenth-century, have been replaced by their modern equivalents. Secondly, the superfluous italics, endemic in most books of the seventeenth-century, have been removed and replaced with a regular text style. Thirdly, a few minor instances of small capitalization have been substituted for regular capitalization.

Readers will notice that in maintaining the integrity of the original publications, the original historic forms of spelling have been retained. More generally, readers will notice both inconsistent and imaginative forms of spelling throughout each book.

This collection has been based on the earliest available edition of each of the publications: *A Discourse of Trade, From England unto the East-Indies: Answering to diverse Objections which are usually made against the same. By T.M.* London: Printed by Nicholas Okes for John Pyper (1621), and *England's Treasure by Forraign Trade. Or, The Ballance of our Forraign Trade is The Rule of Our Treasure.* Written by Thomas Mun, of Lond. Merchant, And now published for the Common good by his Son, John Mun of Bearsted in the County of Kent, Esquire. London, Printed by J.G. for Thomas Clark, and are to be sold at his Shop at the South entrance of the Royal Exchange (1664).

THOMAS MUN
THE COMPLETE WORKS:
ECONOMICS AND TRADE

DISCOVRSE

of Trade,

From England *vnto the* East-Indies:

Answering to diuerse Obiections which are *vsually made against the same.*

By T. M.

LONDON.

Printed by *Nicholas Okes* for *Iohn Pyper.*

1621.

BRIEFE NOTES DIRECTING TO THE SEVERALL PARTS WHICH ARE HANDLED IN THE ANSWERES MADE TO THE FOURE OBJECTIONS AGAINST THE EAST-INDIA TRADE IN THE DISCOURSE FOLLOWING.

BRIEFE NOTES DIRECTING TO THE SEVERALL PARTS WHICH ARE HANDLED IN THE ANSWERES MADE TO THE FOURE OBJECTIONS AGAINST THE EAST-INDIA TRADE IN THE DISCOURSE FOLLOWING.

The parts of the first Objection,

1. In the first part is shewed the necessary use of Drugges, Spices, Indico, Raw-silke and Callicoes.

2. In the second part is declared the great summes of ready monies which are yeerely saved to Christendome in generall, by fetching the wares of the East-Indies directly in shipping from thence.

3. In the third part, is proved, that the Trade from England to the East-Indies doth not consume, but rather greatly increase the generall stocke and Treasure of this Realme.

The parts of the second Objection,

1. In the first part is set forth the noble use of Ships; and that the timber, planke, and other Materials of this Kingdome for the building of Shipping, are neither become scant nor dearer since the East-India Trade beganne.

2. In the second part is shewed the great strength of shipping and warlike provisions, which the East-India Company have alwayes in readinesse for the service of the Kingdome.

The parts of the third Objection,

1. The East-India Trade doth not make victuals deare, but is a meanes to increase our plenty.

2. It breedeth more Mariners then it doth ordinarily consume, and disburtheneth the Kingdome of very many leude people.

3. It hath not destroyed any other Trade or shipping of this Realme, but hath encreased both the one and the other; besides the great addition of it selfe unto the strength and traffique of this Kingdome.

4. It doth not increase the number of the poore of this Realme (as is erroneously supposed). but it doth maintayne and releeve many hundreds of people by their imployments, and

Charitie.

5. It doth save the Kingdome yearely 75000. l. sterling, or thereabouts, of that which it was accustomed to spend in Spices and Indico onely, when they were brought us from Turkey and Lixborne.

The parts of the fourth Objection,

1. The East-India Trade doth not hinder the imployment of his Majesties Mint.

2. The proposition to put downe the East-India Trade is grounded upon idle and false reports, tending to the great hurt of the King and his people.

3. A briefe Narration of a Kingdomes riches, with the foure principall causes which may decay the generall stocke and treasure of this Realme in particular.

A DISCOURSE OF TRADE FROM ENGLAND UNTO THE EAST INDIES:

ANSWERING TO DIVERSE OBJECTIONS WHICH ARE USUALLY MADE AGAINST THE SAME.

A DISCOURSE OF TRADE FROM ENGLAND UNTO THE EAST INDIES:

ANSWERING TO DIVERSE OBJECTIONS WHICH ARE USUALLY MADE AGAINST THE SAME.

The Trade of Merchandize, is not onely that laudable practize whereby the entercourse of Nations is so worthily performed, but also (as I may terme it) the very Touchstone of a kingdomes prosperitie, when therein some certen rules shall be diligently observed. For, as in the estates of private persons, wee may accompt that man to prosper and growe rich, who being possessed of revenues more or lesse, doth accordingly proportion his expences; whereby he may yearelie advance some maintenance for his posteritie. So doth it come to passe in those Kingdomes, which with great care and warinesse doe ever vent out more of their home commodities, then they import and use of forrer wares; for so undoubtedly the remainder must returne to them in treasure. But where a contrarie course is taken, through wantonnesse and riot; to overwaste both forren and domesticke wares; there must the money of necessitie be exported, as the meanes to helpe to furnish such excesse, and so by the corruption of mens conditions and manners, manie rich countries are made exceeding poore, whilest the people thereof, too much affecting their owne enormities, doe lay the fault in something else.

Wherefore, industry to encrease, and frugalitie to maintaine, are the true watchmen of a kingdomes treasury; even when, the force and feare of Princes prohibitions cannot possibly retaine the same.

And therefore, as it is most plaine, that proportion or quantity, must ever be regarded in the importing of forren wares; so must there also be a great respect of qualitie and use; that so, the things most necessarie be first preferred, such as are foode, rayment, and munition for warre and trade; which great blessinges, when any countrie doth sufficiently enioy; the next to be procured are wares, fitting for health, and arts; the last, are those, which serve for our pleasures, and ornament.

Now, forasmuch, as by the providence of almightie God, the Kingdome of England, is endowed with such aboundance of rich commodities, that it hath long enjoyed, not onely great plenty of the things before named, but also, through a superfluitie, hath beene much inriched with treasure brought in from forren parts; which hath given life unto so many worthy trades, amongst which that unto the East-India by name; the report whereof, although it is already spread so famous through the world; yet notwithstanding, heere at home, the clamorous complaints against the same, are growne so loude and generall; that (my selfe being one of the Society it hath much troubled) my private meditations, to conceave the means or true groundes of this confusion. But at the last I resolved my selfe, that the greatest number of these exclaimers, are led away in ignorance; not having as yet, discerned the mysteries of such waightie affaires; some have beene transported with envie, as not participating in the said Societie, or beeing thereby hindred (as they conceive) in some other trade; and others, wholly corrupted in their affections; who whilest they willingly runne into these errors, doe also labour diligently to seduce others; that so, this good and glorie of the Kingdome, might be subverted by our selves, which by the pollicie and strength of Strangers, cannot so easilie beabated; wherefore, it is now a fit time to meete with such injurious courses, by a true Narration of the passages in the said East-India Trade; answering to those severall obiections, which are so commonlie made against the same; That so these misunderstandings and errours may be made knowne unto the whole body of this Kingdome, which at this present time is most worthily represented in those noble assemblies of the high Courts of Parliament; where I hope the worth of this rich Trade, shall be effectually inquired, and so in the end obtaine the credit of an honorable approbation.

I

THE FIRST OBJECTION.

I

THE FIRST OBJECTION.

It were a happie thing for Christendome (say many men) that the Navigation to the East-Indies, by way of the Cape of Good hope, had never bene found out; For in the fleetes of shippes, which are sent thither yearely out of England, Portingall, and the Lowcountries; The gold, silver, and Coyne of Christendome, and particularly of this Kingdome, is exhausted, to buy unnecessarie wares.

THE ANSWERE.

The matter of this Objection is very waighty, and therefore, it ought to be answered fully; the which that I may the better performe, I will divide the same into three parts.

1. In the First, I will consider, the necessarie use of the wares, which are usually brought out of East-India into Europe; namely, Druggs, Spices, Rawsilk, Indico, and

Callicoes.

2. In the Second; I will intimate the manner and meanes, by which the said wares have beene heretofore, and now are brought into Europe.

3. In the Third and last; I will prove, that the Treasure of England, is not consumed, but rather greatly to be increased by the performance of the said Trade.

The First part concerneth the use of Indian wares.

Touching the First; Who is so ignorant, in any famous commonwealth, which will not consent to the moderate use of wholesome Druggs and comfortable Spices? Which have beene so much desired in all times, and by so many Nations; not thereby to surfeit, or to please a lickorish taste (as it often happeneth, with many other fruites and wines) but rather as things most necessarie to preserve their health, and to cure their diseases; even as it is most notably set forth, by some learned men, who have undertaken, to write upon this subject; and therefore; it shall be altogether needlesse heere to discourse upon their severall operations and vertues, seeing that, he that listeth, may be well instructed therein; if hee will peruse the volumes, which are penned by the learned, for the benefit of all those, who shall make use thereof.

Sir Thomas Elyot his Castle of health. Rembert Dodoneus his history of Plants. The French Academy second part, and others.

But if peradventure, it be yet further urged; that divers nations live without the use of Druggs and Spices: the answer is, That either such people know not their vertue; and therefore, suffer much by the want of wares so healthfull; or else, they are most miserable; being without meanes to obtaine the thinges, which they so much want; but sithence I intend to be briefe, I will insist no further upon this point; For the Objecters might aswell deny us the use of Sugars, Wynes, Oyles, Raysons, Figgs, Prunes, and Currandes; and with farre more reason exclaime against Tobacco, Cloth of gold and Silver, Lawnes, Cambricks, Gold and Silver lace, Velvets, Sattens, Taffaeties and divers other manifactures, yearely brought into this Realme, for an infinite value; all which as it is most true, that whilest we consume them, they likewise devoure our wealth; yet neverthelesse, the moderate use of all these wares hath ever suted well with the riches and Majestie of this Kingdome.

But I will come to the Raw-silks and Indico; this being so excellent for the dying of our woollen-cloathes, thereby so much esteemed in so many places of the world; that ornament, together with the great reliefe and maintenance of so many hundreds of poore people; who are continually imployed, in the winding, twisting, and weaving of the same; Insomuch, that by the cherishing of this busines (as his Majestie, for his parte is graciouslie pleased to performe, in remitting the impost of Silke) it may well be hoped, that in short time, industrie will make the arte

France and the Low countries of late yeares do make great quantities of wrought silke, of which wares they were heretofore served from Italy.

to flourish, with no lesse happinesse to this Kingdome, then it hath done (through many ages) to diverse States in Italy, and latelie also to the Kingdome of France, and to the united Provinces of the Lowcountries.

Now as touching the Trade of callicoes, of many sortes, into which the English lately made an entrance; although it cannot bee truly sayd, that this commoditie is profitable for the state of Christendome in generall (in respect they are the manifacture of Infidells, and in great part the weare of Christians) yet neverthelesse, this commoditie, likewise is of singular use, for this common wealth in particular; not onelie therewith to increase the trade into forren parts; but also thereby, greatly to abate the excessive prices of Cambricks, Holland, and other sorts of Linnen-cloath; which daily are brought into this Kingdome, for a verie great summe of mony. And this shall suffice concerning the necessarie use of the Indian wares; In the next place, I will set forth the manner and meanes of their importing into Europe.

France, Italy, South Barbary, and other Countries.

The Second part Sheweth the manner & the meanes by which Indian wares have beene and now are brought into Europe.

It is an errour in those men; who thinke that the Trade of the East-Indies into Europe had first entrance, by the discoverie of the Navigation by the Cape of Good-hope. For many yeares before that time, the traffique of those parts, had his ordinary course by shipping from diverse places in the Indies; yearely resorting with their wares to Mocha in the Red Sea, and Balsera in the

Persian-Gulfe: From both which places, the Merchandize (with great charges) were after transported overland by the Turkes upon Cammells, 50. dayes journey, unto Aleppo in Soria, and to Alexandria in Egypt, (which are the Mart Townes, from whence diverse Nations, as well Turkes, as Christians, doe continually disperse the sayd wares by Sea into the partes of Europe:) by which course, the common enemie of Christendome (the Turke) was Maister of the Trade; which did greatly imploy, and inrich his Subjects, and also fill the Coffers of his owne customes, which he exacted at very high rates; But by the providence of almightie God, the discoverie of that Navigation, to the East-Indies by the Cape of Goodhope (now somuch frequented by the English, Portingalls, and Dutche; and also attempted, by other Christian Kingdomes) hath not onely much decayed the great commerce, betweene the Indians and the Turkes in the Red Sea; and in the Persian Gulfe (to their infinite hurt, and to the great increase of Christian trade,) but it hath also brought a further happinesse unto Christendome in generall, and to the Realme of England in particular, for the venting of more English commodities; and for exporting of a lesse quantitie of silver out of Europe, unto the Infidells, by many thousand poundes yearely, then hath beene accustomed in former times; as I shall prove most plainlie by that which followeth.

Rates upon all sorts of Spices 22. per cent. Rawe-Silkes esteemed about 2. per cent. Indico about 8. per cent.

And First, it will be necessarie to set downe the quantitie of Spices, Indico, and Persian Raw-silke (which is yearely consumed in Europe) and in them all to consider the cost with the charges to lade the same commodities cleare aboard the Shippes from Aleppo; and the like of all the selfe same wares, as they have beene usually dispatched from the Portes of the East-Indies; wherein, will appeare that happinesse, which many doe so much oppose; especially our owne Countrie-men, under the gilded tearmes of the Common-wealth; whilest beeing indeed either ignorant, or ill affected, they doe not onelie grosly erre themselves, but also cause others to hinder as much as in them lieth, the glorie and well-fare of this Kingdome; but leaving them, I will set downe the said wares, in their quantitie and prizes as followeth; and first,

Such people as affect not the good of this Kingdome.

The quantitie of Spice, Indico, and Persian Raw-Silke, yeerely consumed in Europe.

At Allepo.

lbs.	*l.*	*s.*	*d.*
6000000. of Pepper, cost with charges at Aleppo at 2.s the lb.	*600000*	*00*	*00*
450000. of Cloves at 4s. 9d. the pound	*106875*	*10*	*00*
150000. of Mace at 4s. 9d. the pound	*35626*	*00*	*00*
400000. of Nutmegs, at 2s. 4d. the pound	*46666*	*13*	*04*
350000. of Indico at 4s. 4d. the pound	*75833*	*06*	*08*
1000000. of Persia raw silke at 12s. the pound	*600000*	*00*	*00*
	1465001	*10*	*00*

Now followeth the same wares both for quantitie and qualitie at their several prizes as they are to be bought and laden cleare of charges.

In the East-Indies.

lbs.	*l.*	*s.*	*d.*
6000000. of Pepper cost with charges in India 2s. 0½d. the pound	*62500*	*00*	*00*
450000. Cloves at 9d. the pound.	*16875*	*00*	*00*
150000. Maces at 8d. the pound	*5000*	*00*	*00*
400000. Nutmegs at 4d. the pound	*6666*	*00*	*00*
350000. Indico at 14d. the pound	*20416*	*12*	*04*
1000000. Persia Raw-silke at 8s. the pound	*400000*	*00*	*00*
	511458	*05*	*08*

So that by the substance, and summes of these accompts, it doth plainely appeare, that the buying of the said quantitie of Raw-silkes, Indico, and Spices, may be performed in the Indies, for neare one third part of the ready moneyes, which were accustomed to be sent into Turkey to provide the same; So that there will bee saved everie yeere the value of 953543. l. 4s. 4d. starling of readie moneyes, that heretofore hath beene exported out of Christendome into Turkey; which is a matter of such note and consequence, that it may seeme incredible, before the circumstance be dulie considered; and therefore least I should leave the matter in doubt, it is requisite; that I

The exportation of the value of 953543. l. starling out of Christendome into Turkey yeerely saved.

doe make an explanation of some particulars.

And principallie, it must not bee conceived, that this great advantage, which hath beene spoken of, is onely the Merchants gaine; for the Common-wealth of Christendome, hath a very great part thereof in the cheapnes of the wares; as shall be (God willing) proved hereafter in his due place.

Secondly, the time of the Merchants forbearance, and interest, is verie long: his adventure and assurance much dearer; his charges of shipping, victuals, Marriners, and factors their wages, far greater, then by the voyage into Turkey for the same wares; so that the former great difference must be understood in these particulers; whereby we may perceive to our comfort, that the Materialls of the kingdome, and the imployments of the subjects (in liew of readie moneies) becomes a verie great part of the price which is paid for the said Indian wares; which cannot hurt the State (as some erroniously suppose) but greatly helpe it, as I shall better prove in that which followeth.

Instance only, that ten shillings imployed in Pepper in the East-Indies, will require thirty and five shillings for all charges whatsoever to deliver it in London.

First therefore, I shew for an undoubted truth, That the Persians, Moores, and Indians, who trade with the Turkes, at Aleppo, Mocha, and Alexandria, for Raw-silkes, Drugs, Spices, Indico and Callicoes; have alwaies made, and still doe make, their returnes in readie money: for other wares, there are but few which they desire from forren partes; some Chamblets, Corrall, wrought silke, woollen-cloth, with some trifles, they doe yearely vent in all, not for above 40. or 50. thousand pounds starling; which is no valuable summ in respect of that wealth which is carried from Aleppo and Constantinople into Persia for Raw-silkes, when least, 500000. poundes starling Per annum: and from Mocha about 600000. pounds starling (likewise yearely into India) for returne of Callicoes, Drugs, Sugar, Rice, Tobacco, and diverse other things. So here is still a very great Commerce maintained betweene those Infidels; not onely for the Callicoes of many sortes, and other wares (which concerne their owne use) but also for the Raw-silkes of Persia, which are altogether transported into Christendome.

The great Summes of money which the Persians and the Indians carrie yeerely out of Turkey.

How worthy an enterprise is it therefore in the English East-India Companie? by whose endeavours, there is now good hope to turne a great part of this wealthy Trade into England, by shipping directile from the Persian-Gulfe, whereby the imployments, traffique, and Customes of the Turkes, may be still more and more impaired; & the generall Treasure of Christendome much lesse consumed; as is alreadie performed for the businesse of Spices and Indico.

The East-India Companie doe endeavour to bring the Raw-Silkes from Persia directly by Sea.

And who shall then doubt our want of Silver to mainetaine the Trade? if by this way wee doe obtaine the Silke, which with more advantage and conveniencie, wil draw the money to this Mart, then it hath beene heeretofore conveyed unto those remote dominions of the Turke.

And least peradventure it should be thought, that the traffique in those parts by the Christians for the Persian Silke, is performed by change for other wares, or by the money which proceedeth of the sales of many rich commodities, which yeerely they sell at Aleppo, Alexandria, Constantinople, and these parts.

The answere is, that neither the Venetians, French, nor Dutche, doe vent so much of their owne Country commodities in those partes, as doe provide their necessarie wants of the proper wares of Turkes: such, as are the fine Raw-silke, made in Soria, Chamblets, Grogerans, Cotten-woolles, Cotten-yarne, Gaules, Flax, Hempe, Fleece-woolls, Rice, Hides, Waxe, & diverse other things; so that still their raw-silkes of Persia, must be bought with ready mony. Only the English have more advantage then any other Nation in this kinde, for they vent so great a quantitie of broade-cloathes, tinne, and other English commodities, that the proceede thereof, doth not only provide a sufficient quantitie of part of the said Turkish wares (which fit their use,) but also a proportion of about 300. great balles of Persia Raw-silke yearely.

Marcellis sendeth yeerely to Aleppo & Alexandria at least 500000.l. sterling, and little or no wares. Venice sendes about the value of 100000.l. and a great value in wares. The Lowcountries sends about the value of 50000.l. sterling moneys, and little wares. Messina 25000.l. in ready money.

And if in any yeare, they chance to buy a greater quantitie of silke, then must and do they furnish the same in ready monies from the Portes of Marcellis, Genouay, Ligorne,

Venice, or the Netherlandes. Neither are these the onely meanes, whereby the Empire of the Turke is so abundantly stored with Gold and Silver, to the performance of the Indian-trade. For, many are the Christian shippes, which yearely lade with corne for ready monies in the Archipelago; Great is the commerce from Poland, Hungarie, and Germany, with Gold and Dollers, for Chamblets, Grogerans, and other things: But that which is very remarkable, is the great quantitie of gold & some silver coyned in Grand-Cairo, which by two severall Carravans (in bullion) is yearely brought thither from the Abissians countrie in Ethiopia, for returne of many rich commodities, as Velvets, Sattens, Cloth of Gold, Taffaties, Woollen-cloath: polished Corrall, and other things.

Abissians a people in Ethiopia whose influence hath made them dull, lazy, and without artes; enjoying divers Mines of Gold and one of Silver, which doe procure their wants of forren wares.

Thus by the coherence of the Turkish-Trade with the Christians, Persians, and Indians, I have shewed both the manner and the meanes, whereby the East-Indian wares have beene heretofore, and yet are, in part, procured into Christendome. But least it should seeme incredible, that the Turke would let so great a Masse of Treasure yeerly to passe his Dominions, to the Indians and to the Persians his professed enemies: I will make the matter yet more plaine.

And First, concerning the Raw-silkes, it is alreadie shewed, that hee hath the money from the Christians, besides the benefit he reapeth in their customes, with great implployments also for his Subjects. And for the Callicoes (his whole Empire having litle or no other meanes for Linnen) he can not possibly be without them, although it hath, & doth greatly exhaust his treasure; neither doth he gaine any manufacture by the same, as the Christians have alwayes done by the Raw-silke, to the great reliefe of innumerable poore people, so much provided for, by the pollicie of all well governed and flourishing common-wealths: As by this occasion, and in a businesse of the like kind, I may instance the States of Genouay, Florence, and Luca; who for the maintenance of Artes and Trade, doe provide Raw-silkes out of Sicilia for the value of 500000. poundes starling at least yearlie; and for the payment thereof they doe vent at Naples, Palermo, Messina, and those parts a certaine quantitie of Florence-Rashes and some other wares, for about 150000. pounds starling per annum; So the rest, being 350000.l. sterling, is supplyed all in readie moneies; which treasure they doe willingly forsake, to procure their Trade; for experience hath taught them that Trade is their imployment, and doth returne them treasure; for by those silkes (being wrought, transported & sould at Franckforde and other Marts) they have the better meanes, to furnish their contracts with the King of Spaine in Flanders; and so from Spaine the Silver must returne againe to Italy. But if I should runne out in this and other particulars (fitting our

Turkey hath litle meanes for Linnen but onely from India.

The proceedings of some States in Italy for the maintenance of Artes.

The ready moneys which are yearely carried from some States of Italy into Sicilia.

purpose) it would make me too tedious, and so carrie me beyond my ayme, which is to be briefe.

Wherefore, I will proceede to cleare some doubts, in those men, who perhaps not having the knowledge of occurrents in forren partes, might thinke, that neither Venice, nor Marcellis have the meanes or yet the mindes, to exporte such great Sommes of readie monyes, yearely out of those Dominions; especially Marcellis being a part of France, where neighbourhoode doth daily tell us, that gold and Silver, may not be conveied out of that Kingdome, for any valuable Somme, more then is permitted for the necessarie use of Travellers; Yet neverthelesse experience hath likewise taught us, that for the effecting of those Trades (whereof wee now speake, and which they esteeme so much) there is a free extraction out of the sayd places, of moneyes both gold and silver; whereof with them there is no want; for, the sayd wares doe procure it abundantly.

How Marcellis and Venice are furnished with ready moneys.

First, to Marcellis, it commeth not onely from Genouay, Ligorne, Cartagenia, Malliga, and many other Porte townes of Spaine and Itally, but also from Parris, Roane, Sainct Malloes, Tolouse, Rochell, Deepe, and other Cities of France; who want not meanes to have great store of Rialls, and Dallers from Spaine & Germany.

And in like manner, the Venetians distributing the sayd Raw-silkes, and other wares into the severall States of Itally, Germany, and Hungarie, (who have but few commodities fitting their barter or exchange: but onely monyes) are therewith aboundantly served; For the mynes of Hungarie and Germany affoord good quantitie of Gold and Silver; And likewise the States of Itally, especiallie Genouay, Florence, and Millane, have ever store of Rialls out of Spaine in satisfaction of many great disbursments, which those Merchantes make for that King in his occasions of Itally and Flanders; of all which, I might make a large discourse, but I conceave I have sayd sufficient, to shew how the trade of the EastIndies hath beene, and now is brought into Christendome generally: what money is yearely sent out; by whom; and the possibilitie, or meanes which they have to performe it. I will therefore in the next place, satisfie the Objectors; that it is not the East-India Trade, which wasteth the Gold, and Silver, Coyne, or other treasure of this kingdome in particular.

The Italyan Merchants doe furnish the king of Spaine with money in Italy and Flanders.

For first, who knoweth not, that gold in the East-Indies hath no ratable price with Silver? Neither hath the Silver coyne of England any equall value with the Spanish Rialls according to their severall prices here; Besides that, his Majestie hath not authorized the East-India Companie, to send away any part of this kingdomes Coyne either Gold, or Silver; but onely a certaine limited summe of forren Silver yearlie; which as they

The third part doth shew how the East-India Trade doth enrich this Kingdome.

dare not exceede, so never have they as yet accomplished the same.

For it doth plainely appeare in their bookes; that from the originall and first foundation of the Trade, in Anno 1601. untill the moneth of July, Anno 1620. they have shipped away onely 548090.l. sterling in Spanish Rialls, and some Dollers; whereas, by licence, they might have exported in that time 720000.l. sterling.

How much money and wares the East-India Company have sent forth ever sithence the beginning of this Trade.

Also they have laden away in the same tearme of xix yeares, out of this Kingdome 292286.l. sterling in Broad-clothes, Kersies, Lead, Tinne, with some other English and forren commodities; which is a good Addition, and vent of our wares, into such remote places; where heretofore they have had no utterance at all.

And note, I pray you, how time and industrie hath bettered this Trade, when in the last three yeares, there hath beene sent more wares to the Indies, then in the xvi. yeares before; and yet our expectation is not at the highest; for those new borne Trades within the Red Sea, and in the Persian Gulfe, doe bid us hope for better things, as lately by letters from Spahan, we understand of great quantity of Raw silke prepared by the English factors, which (by Gods assistance) wee may expect here about the Moneth of August next; with encouragement also, to vent our English cloth, and Kersies in good quantities; the like of Iron, Tinne, and other things; whereof

The vent of English wares increased in the Indies.

experience (of those alreadie sould) hath given us sufficient approbation of their validitie.

Our stock may be much increased by Trade from Port to Porte in the Indies.

And now (omitting much matter which might be written touching the discoveries of other Trades from one Kingdome or port to another, in the Indies: with the commodities thereof, whereby the imployment of our shippes, together with the stocke of money and goodes which is sent out of England in them, may be much increased) I will draw to a conclusion of the point in hand; and shewe, That whatsoever Summes of forren readie monyes are yearely sent from hence into the East-Indies, His Majestie in the letters Pattents graunted to that Company, hath notwithstanding with singular Care provided, that the brethren of the Company, shall yearely bring in as much silver, as they send forth; which hath beene alwayes truly performed, with an overplus, to the increase of this Kingdomes treasure: Neither is it likelie, that the money which is thus contracted for, by the Companie at certaine prices, and to be delivered them at times appointed, would bee otherwise brought into England, but onely by vertue and performance of the said contracts; for without this assurance of Vent, together with a good price for the said monyes, the Merchants would undoubtedly make their returnes in other wares; the use and extraordinarie consume whereof, would be found lesse profittable to the Commonwealth, when the matter should be duly considered, as

The moneys sent to the Indies is all forren Coyne.

The East-India Companie are obliged to bring in as much money as they carry out of the Realme.

Tobacco, Raysons, Oyles, and Wines, whereof there is no want, but rather too much Smoake.

I shall yet further endeavour to demonstrate.

And here I will suppose, That the East-India Company may shippe out yearely 100000.l. starling (more or lesse) as occasion may be offered; yet it is most certaine, that the Trade being thus driven with such sums of ready moneys, it will not decay but rather much increase the treasure of the kingdome: which to prove, I will briefely set downe the substance of the English Trade unto the East-Indies, concerning the quantitie of the severall sortes of wares, to be yearely bought there and sould here; with the usual prices given for them in both places. And first, I will beginne with their Coste and charges laden cleare aboard the shippes in the East-Indies.

A proportion of such Trade as is hoped yeerely to be brought into this Realme from East-India.

In the East-Indies.

lbs.	*l.*	*s.*	*d.*
2500000 lbs. of Pepper at 2.d. ob. the pound.	*26041*	*13*	*04*
150000 of Cloves at 9.d. the pound.	*5626*	*00*	*00*
150000 of Nutmegs at 4.d. the pound.	*2500*	*00*	*00*
50000 of Maces at 8.d. the pound.	*16666*	*13*	*04*
200000 of Indico at 14.d. the pound.	*11666*	*13*	*04*
107140 of China Raw silkes at 7.s. the pound.	*37499*	*00*	*00*
50000 of Callicoes of severall sorts, rated at 7.s. the peece one with another.	*15000*	*00*	*00*
	100000	*00*	*00*

All the sayd Merchandize have beene often experienced, or bought at or about the prices above written; & we doe hope for our parts (besides the Trade of Raw-silkes from Persia) yearely, to lade from the Indies, such quantitie of the severall sortes of wares as are here set downe (if it shall please his Majestie, to protect and defend us concerning the Articles of agreement made with the Dutche, that they may not violate any of them to our hindrance or damage) all which wares in England will yeelde (as I doe conceave) the prizes hereafter following, Viz.

In England.

lbs.	*l.*	*s.*	*d.*
2500000 lbs. of Pepper at 20.d. the pound.	*208333*	*06*	*08*
150000 of Cloves at 6.s. the pound.	*45000*	*00*	*00*
150000 of Nutmegs at 2.s. 6.d. the pound.	*18750*	*00*	*00*
50000 of Mace at 6.s. the pound.	*15000*	*00*	*00*
200000 of Indico at 5.s. the pound.	*50000*	*00*	*00*
107140 of China Raw silkes at 20.s. the pound.	*107140*	*00*	*00*
50000 peeces of Callicoes of severall sorts, rated at 20.s. the peece one with another.	*50000*	*00*	*00*
	494223	*06*	*08*

How much the kingdomes stocke may increase yeerely by trading to the East-Indies.

So that here would be our owne money againe; and more, the somme of 394223.l. 06.s. 08.d. advanced towards the generall stocke of the Kingdome. For although the East-India Company shall disburse the greatest part of the sayd somme advanced unto his Majestie for custome and impost; and also unto the Factors, Officers, and Marriners, for wages, together with the cost of shipping, Victualls, Munitions, Assurance and the like; yet all these (the Materialls of shipping only excepted) are but transmutations, and no consumption of the Kingdomes stocke.

2500. Tonnes of shipping wil lade home all the wares afore written from the East-Indies. And the materialls of the said shipping (unwrought) is worth about 15000.l. sterling.

But if any man object, and say, that the sayd commodities being brought into England (as is before written) they are either consumed in the land, or being transported into forren partes, they are changed into other wares; So that still we want our 100000.l. in readie money:

1. The answere is; first, that in the occasion of this dispute, wee must conceave the said wares to be of no use for this kingdom, but onely for so much, as doe concerne the Trade thereof.

2. And secondly, in the said Trade, wee must consider, that although the said goodes be sent out, and returned home in other wares from forren partes; yet still, they are negotiated to the increase of the said stocke, and for the imployment of the subjects.

3. Lastly, if there bee a resolution to determine and end the businesse: who doubteth, that the whole value, may not be

India wares wil bring readie moneys into the Realme.

presently returned hither in readie moneyes? For in Italy, Turkey, and other places, where they are most vendible to profit, there likewise is the money free to be exported at all times and by whomsoever.

We have no other meanes to procure Treasure but by Trade and Merchandize.

And as it is most certen, that some other Merchandize, sent out of this Kingdome were the meanes to bring in the 100000.l. in readie moneyes, which is here supposed to be sent and imployed in the East-Indies (as aforesaid) so likewise, there is the same power in these Indian wares, to procure other sommes of ready moneyes, to be brought into this kingdome: For let no man doubt, but that money doth attend Merchandize, for money is the prize of wares, and wares are the proper use of money; so that their Coherence is unseparable. And if the French and the Venetians, made any doubt of this, they would not so willingly permit the vallue of 600000.l. sterling, or more in Spanish Rialls and Dollers, yearely to be carried out of their Dominions into Turkey: whereof three quarter partes at least are imployed, onely for the buying of Persia Raw-silkes, which commoditie doth presently enable them with readie money from diverse other States to performe the Trade; whereby their wealth doth much increase, and their people are greatly imployed. So to conclude this point, I will onely add, that the East-India Trade alone (although it be driven in no amplier manner then is afore written) is a meanes to

The French and the Venetians send the vallue of 600000.l. sterling yeerely in ready money into Turkey.

Trade maketh some States very rich which have little other meanes.

bring more treasure into this Realme then al the other trades of this kingdome (as they are now mannaged) being put together.

For if the rule be true, that when the value of our commodyties exported doth overballance the worth of all those forraigne wares which are imported and consumed in this Kingdome, then the remaynder of our stock which is sent forth, must of necessitie returne to us in Treasure. I am confident that upon a diligent and true inquiry it will be found, that the overballance of all our other trades together will not amount unto so great a summe of money as the East-India Trade alone doth over ballance in this kinde.

If the generall Trade of this Kingdome doth export a greater value in wares then it doth import yearely, then doth our treasure increase.

And to make the matter yet more plaine, whereas it is already said that 100000.l. in money exported may import about the value of 500000. poundes sterling, in wares from the East-Indies, wee must understand that part thereof to bee properly called our importation that this Realme doth consume, which is about the value of 120000. pounds sterling yeerely. So the remainder being 380000.l. is matter exported into forraine parts in the nature of our Cloath, Lead, Tinne, or any other native commodities, to the great increase of this Kingdomes stocke, and that also in so much treasure, so farre as the East-India Trade can be rightly understood to subsist in this particular.

The trade to the East-Indies may be said to export 480000 poundes and to importe 120000.l. yearely. So the overballance is 360000 pounds sterling.

For as all humane actions haue their termination and ends, so likewise there must

Every action ought especially to be considered in his ende.

be an end assigned unto the affayres of the East-Indies; which are then truely sayd to be finished, when this Realme is served, and the remaynder of those wares which are sent from hence beyond the Seas, sould there, and converted into money; which likewise from thence may bee brought away freely & without the danger of Law or prohibition.

The East-Indian wares which were sent beyond the seas, are sould and have their finall end in money, which might be brought into this Realme in that kind, if our other Trades did not divert the same.

Forasmuch therefore as it is well knowne to many men, that monyes are thus procured by the Sales of Indian wares to profit, in the partes of Turkey, and at Ligorne, Genouay, the Netherlands, Marcellis, and other places: yet notwithstanding if all the said coine, or any part thereof should be diverted from this Realme by some other new imployments or affaires, it must neverthelesse be granted, that the sayd India wares had their finall end in moneies. But I will cease to heape up any more arguments, to prove a matter which is alreadie made so plaine; wherefore leaving this Objection, I will endeavour to give Answere to the next.

II

THE SECOND OBJECTION.

II

THE SECOND OBJECTION.

The timber, Plancke, and other materialls, for making of shipping, is exceedinglie Wasted, and made dearer, by the building of so many great Shippes, as are yearely sent to Trade in the East-Indies; and yet the State hath no use of any of them upon occasion. For either they are not here; or else they come home verie weake, and unserviceable.

THE ANSWERE.

This East-India Trade seemeth to be borne and brought up an Unthrift, for it wasteth and consumeth all; Neither doth it good to any.

But the Objection, in some part is
very weake:
And in the rest it is mistaken.

For first, concerning the weaknesse thereof; *The first part concerneth the folly of the Objection.*

would men have us to keepe our woods and goodly trees to looke upon? they might as well forbid the working of our woolls, & sending forth our cloth to forren partes; for both are meanes alike, to procure the necessarie wares, which this Kingdome wanteth. Doe they not knowe that trees doe live and growe; and being great, they have a time to dye and rot, if oportunitie make no better use of them? and what more noble or profitable use then goodly Ships for Trade & warre? are they not our barns for wealth and plentie, serving as walles and Bulwarkes for our peace and happines? Doe not their yearely buildings maintaine many hundred poore people, and greatlie increase the number of those Artesmen which are so needfull for this common wealth?

The providence of the East-India company for timber & Planke.

And is not all this good performed also (with great providence) by bringing in yearelie store of Tymber, and other provisions from Ireland? Why then, where is the great wast and dearnesse? I am sure, the East-India Company findes it not; for whereas they do only buy their provisions in Hampshire, Essex, Kent, and Barkeshire, in all which places they now may have both Timber, Planks, Sheathing boards, Trenalls, and the like, both for goodnesse and price, as cheape (yea better cheape) then they have bin this fifteene yeares; and likewise in all that course of time their bookes doe plainely shew that those wares have never varied much; for if they have risen any smal matter in one yeare they have

The East-India Trade hath not indeared the materialls which serve to make shippes.

fallen as much the next. And yet I pray you observe (besides the East-India Companies buildings) the many goodlie shippes, which are daily made for other private Merchants (such as England never had before:) & that which is most remarkable, is, the continuall late buildings of his Majestie, thereby yearely adding more strength and glory of great Shippes, to his Royall and matchlesse Navy; so that, here wee see this supposed wast and want is not considerable.

The Second Part sheweth the mistaking in the Objection.

Yea but, say they, the East-India Shippes are never here, to serve the Kingdome upon occasion: Or if they beat home, they are weake, and unfit for service.

The warlike provision which the East-India Company keepe in store.

In trade of Merchandize our Shippes must goe and come, they are not made to stay at home; yet neverthelesse, the East-India companie are well prepared at all times, to serve his Majestie, and his Kingdomes, with many warlike provisions, which they alwayes keep in store; such as Timber, Planks, Iron-workes, Masts, Cordage, Anchors, Caske, Ordinance, Powder, Shot, Victualls readie packed, Wine, Sider, and a world of other things, fitting the present building, repairing and dispatch of Shippes to Sea; as may bee plentifullie seene in their yardes and storehouses at Deptforde, and more especiallie in those at Blackewalle; which are growne so famous, that they are daily visited & viewed by strangers, as well Embassadors, as others; to their great admiration of his Majesties strength, & glory,

His Majesties strength in the East-India Company alone.

in one only Company of his Merchants, able at short warning to set forth a fleet of Ships of great force & power.

For it is well knowne to al men who please truely to be informed, That the East-India Companie (besides their fleetes of Shippes going and comming, & also abiding in the Indies) are continuallie building, repairing, rigging, victualling, and furnishing to Sea, with all provision needefull for such a long voyage, some 7. or 8. great shippes yearelie; which are to be seene at an Anchor in the River of Thames in a great forwardnes some 5. or 6. moneths together, before they commonly depart for the Indies, which is about the moneth of March: & they are no sooner got off from the coast of England, but shortly after, is the season of our ships to returne from the Indies; who come not home so weake as some would have them; for how often hath experience bin made of our shippes which have performed 2. or 3. several voyages to the East-Indies? Yet at their returne, they have beene indocked, new trimmed and lanched out againe, fitted for the like voyages, in lesse then 2. moneths. But it will be needlesse to spend any more time in shewing the errors of this 2. Objection: therefore I will rather come to the handling of that which followeth.

The shippes which returne from the East-Indies home, may be repayred in a very short time.

III

THE THIRD OBJECTION.

III

THE THIRD OBJECTION.

The voyages to the East Indies doe greatly consume our victuals, and our Marriners: leaving many poore widdowes and children unrelieved; Besides, that many Ships are yearely sent forth to the East Indies, and few we see as yet returned; Also, this Trade hath greatly decayed the Traffique and shipping, which were wont to be imployed into the Streights: And yet the said Trade of the East Indies, is found very unprofitable to the Adventurers: Neither doth the Common-wealth finde any benefit by the cheapenesse of Spice and Indico, more then in times past.

THE ANSWER.

Why, what a world of mischiefes have we heere?

1. Dearth.
2. Mortalitie.
3. Destruction.

4. Beggerie.
5. And never a whit the neere.

A verie Teame of calamities, drawing on to misery; is it not then high time to seeke a remedy? Yes verily, and it will be easily done, because these evils never were (as yet at least) procured by the East India Trade, as I shall shew, by answering all the parts in order as they stand: and first of Dearth.

The first Part concerneth Dearth.

It is both naturall and just, that every Kingdome, State, or Common-wealth, should feede and cherish up the Native people of all degrees and conditions whatsoever, to their preservation of life and health, with such meanes and moderation, as their plentie shall affoord; and this is not onely due to them in the time of their aboad at home, but also upon all occasions of voyages into other Countries beyond the Seas, wherein they shall be imployed for their owne maintenance, and for the good of the Common-wealth.

The manner how the East India Company do victuall their ships.

Now therefore concerning the provision of victuals (which in this Kingdome is yearely prepared for the setting forth of those Ships which saile to the East Indies,) it is well knowen to many men, that it is alwaies proportioned, for about eighteene months; whereas commonly the voyages prove a yeare longer, so that this over-plus of time, is furnished with victuals of forreine parts.

And likewise for the Bread and Bisket which is shipped from hence; hath it not alwaies beene made of French Corne, purposly brought over hither (and that at a deare rate) onely to preserve the plentie of owne graine? untill now of latedaies that the Farmers heere beginne to cry out and say, that the cheapnesse of Corne doth disinable them to pay their deare Rents: Thus doe the East India Company every way accommodate their proceedings for the good of the Kingdome. And further concerning their Drinke, is it not a very great part water? Some Wine and Sider, and but little Beere.

Also the Flesh they eate, is Beefe and Porke, and that onely for three daies in a weeke; the rest of their victuals is Fish, some Butter, Cheese, Pease, Oatemale, and other things; all which is proportioned into a very sparing dyet to everie man by allowance: so that heere is no excesse nor ryot, or any other meanes to make our victuals scant and deare, as is by some erroniously supposed; but rather by this course of life, our plentie is much advanced. And so I will give answer to the next part which is mortalitie, and great decay of Marriners.

The Second Part concerneth Mortality.

The life of man is so pretious, that it ought not lightly to be exposed to dangers; And yet we know, that the whole course of our life, is nothing but a passage unto Death; wherein one can neither stay nor slacke his pace, but all men runne in one manner, and in one celeritie; The shorter liver runnes his course no faster then the long, both have a like passage of time; howbeit, the first hath not so farre to runne as the later.

Now, it is this length of life which Nature seekes, and States likewise endevour to preserve in worthy men; but none are accounted so worthy in this nature, save onely they, who labour in their vocations and functions, both for the publique good, and for their private benefit.

Good Marriners are accounted worthy men in a Commonwealth.

Thus may we esteeme our good Marriners, to be of no small use unto this Common-wealth: but take them from their laudable and accustomed imployments, for want of voyages to Sea; wee see what desperate courses they doe then attempt, by joyning, even with Turkes and Infidels, to rob and spoyle all Christian Nations; so that we may conclude, we must not onely breed up Marriners, but also seeke by Trade, to give them a maintenance.

Well, all this is true, but (say they) the East India Company doth neither breed nor maintaine, but destroy the wonted number of our Marriners.

How can this be, when it is most certaine, that England (besides the East India fleets) had never yet more shipping then at this present? neither do any of them stay at home for want of Marriners, no, not at this time, when many hundred Saylers are employed in extraordinary service, for his Majestie in a Royall fleete of ships, now at Sea: besides those great numbers of our best Marriners, which have beene and dayly are wasted and taken prisoners by the Turkes; so where is this want, or what is our misery more then the want of true information in them that are so ill perswaded of our company?

Is it not certaine, that as the East India voyages are long, so likewise in Natures course many should die by length of time, although they stayd at home? And to recompence the losse of those that dye, doe not the East India company with great providence, yearly ship out at least 400. Landmen in their fleets, which in one voyage prove good Marriners to serve the Kingdome and Common wealth, unto which many of them were a burthen before they obtained this employment? And thus is the Kingdome purged of desperate and unruly people, who being kept in awe by the good discipline at Sea, do often change their former course of life, and so advance their fortunes.

The breeding of 400 Marriners yearely. Besides that the feare of a few mens death ought not to overthrow or hinder the performance of honorable actions for the service of the King and commonwealth.

Neither indeed are these voyages so dangerous and mortall, as is reported; for how many of our Ships, have gone and come from the East Indies, without the losse of five men in a hundreth? Others againe have had worse successe in the first beginning, when the seasons, the places, and their contagions were not so well knowne unto us; yet time hath taught us many things, both for the preservation of health, and speedier performance of our voyage then heretofore. But the Method of my discourse bids me

Our Marriners owne disordered life is that which killeth many of them.

write more of this in the next part, which is destruction; and this I must divide into two parts.

In the first I will consider the want of divers ships sent to the East Indies, which are wasted there.

And in the second, I will answer the supposed overthrow of the Turkie trade, together with much of our shipping which were wont to bee employed thither.

The third Part concernes the decay of shipping which have beene sent to the Indies.

First therefore concerning the decay of our ships in the Indies, it cannot bee denyed, but there hath been great spoyle of them in these three last yeares; not by the dangers of the Seas, or by the strength of enemies; but by unkind and unexspected quarrels with our neighbours the Hollanders, who have taken and surprised twelve of our ships at severall times, and in sundry places, to our unspeakeable losse and hinderance; together with the death of many of our worthyest Marriners, who have beene slaine and died prisoners under their hands: and this hath so much the more encreased the rumour of their mortality: Neither list I here to aggravate the fact, more then thus, briefly to give answere to the objection: for our late union with the Dutch, doth promise a double recompence of gain in time to come.

Our troubles with the Dutch.

And they who make this Trade so poore and unprofitable, are much mistaken in the reckoning; for the present losses which causeth many adventurers so much to despaire, is not in the substance of the Trade, but by the evill accidents which have befalne the same: & to make this pointmore plain, I must yet declare some other particulars: in which I will endeavour very briefly to set downe the summe of the whole businesse, which the English hath hitherto performed in the East Indies.

The summe of the affaires to the East Indies ever since the Trade began.

First, therefore I doe observe that since the beginning of this Trade, untill the Moneth of July last Anno 1620. there have beene sent thither 79. ships in severall voyages, whereof 34. are already come home in safety richly laden. 4. have been worne out by long service, from Port to Port in the Indies: two were overwhelmed in the trimming there: 6. have beene cast away by the perils of the Seas; 12. have beene taken and surprized by the Dutch, whereof divers will be wasted, and little worth before they be restored: and 21. good ships do still remaine in the Indies. So this is a true account of our ships.

Account of all the money and goods which hath been sent to the East Indies ever since the beginning of the Trade.

And next concerning our stocke, it is a certaine truth, that in all in the sayde ships there hath beene sent out in ready money as well out of this Realme, as from all other places wheresoever beyond the Sea (which hath not been landed in this Kingdom) the vallue of 548090. pounds sterling in forraine coine; and together with the sayd money there hath beene shipped the value of 292286. pounds sterling in sundry sorts of English and forraine commodities; all which moneys and wares amounting vnto 840376. pounds, have been disposed, as hereafter followeth.

First, there hath been lost 31079. pounds sterling, in the 6. ships which are cast away: and in the 34. ships, which are returned in safety, there hath beene brought home 356288. pounds sterling in divers sorts of wares, which have produced here in England towards the generall stocke there of 1914600.l. sterling; for the charges arising here, is but a change of effects from one to another, as hath beene sayde before in this discourse: So there ought to remaine in the Indies, to be speedily returned hither, 484088. pounds: neither can we conceive that our charges and troubles with the Dutch, wil have wasted more then the odd 84088. pounds sterling: so that I am confident, that there yet remaineth 400000. pounds sterling of good estate, for both the joynt stockes. And what a great value of Indian goods this sum of money may (by Gods blessing) shortly return in our ships, which are there ready to bring them, the example here doth teach us to make up the reckoning, So that notwithstanding our great charges of discoveries, our losses by the danger of the Seas, our quarrels & infinite hindrance by the Dutch: yet heer the kingdome hath, and shall have her stock againe with a very great encrease, although the Merchants gaines concerning the two joynt stocks will prove but poore, in respect of the former voyages, which have not had the like hindrance.

356288.l. sterling hath been returned from the East Indies which did produce here towards charges 1914600.l. sterling.

There remains yet in the East Indies to be returned home from thence about 400000.l. starling.

And thus in a few lines may be seene, much matter truly collected with some paines, out of the divers volumes of the East Indian Bookes.

Concerning the decay of shipping and Trade into Turkey.

Now concerning the decay of Trade and shipping, which were wont to be imployed into Turkey, I doubt, that in time it will likewise be affirmed, that the East India Company, have hindred the vent of our white Cloath in the Netherlands, which to report were a verie strange thing. But (praised be God) to our comfort, we see the great increase of goodly Ships, daily built and imployed, by the Turkey Merchants with vent of more of our English Cloath (by one third part at least) then in times before the East India Trade began.

Yea, but (say they) we have lost the trade of Spices, and Indico, from Aleppo into England.

Well, I grant they have; yet the Kingdome hath found it with more profit by another way; and they likewise are recompenced with a greater Trade, by the exporting from hence of the selfe-same commodities into Italy, Turkey, and other places: neither can it be lesse profitable for this Kingdome, to turne the Trade of Raw-silkes from Aleppo, and to bring them from the Persian gulfe, with one third part lesse money, then it doth now cost in Turkey; Besides, that by this meanes, the money proceeding of our English Cloath, Tin, and other wares in Turkey (not finding commodities fitting to returne for England) would undoubtedly be brought home in Gold, as it hath beene performed heretofore, when by superfluitie of stocke sent from hence in Spice, together with our English wares; the Merchants (being thereby furnished with a sufficient quantity of Turkish commodities) brought home the remainder of their stock of those yeares in gold for a great value.

The Turkey Merchants can and will justify this truth.

Thus doth it plainely appeare, that these revolutions of Trades, have and doe turne to the good of the Commonwealth; neither hath the affayres of the East Indies impaired or decayed any other Trade, Shipping or Marriners of this Realme; but hath mightily increased them all in it selfe. Wherefore let us now take a view of this noble addition of the kingdomes strength and glory.

But this I must not doe, by setting downe the number of our English shipping now in the Indies, or lately gone that way; for they have beene heaped thither, these three last yeares together without returne, save onely five ships in all that time; the rest have beene kept there to oppose the furie of the Dutch; but now we are at union, we shall (by Gods assistance) daily exspect divers great ships with returnes.

The strength of the East India ships.

And for the future time, this Trade I do conceive, will royally maintayne ten thousand tuns of shipping continually: (That is to say) going, and returning, and abiding there in the Indies; which said shipping will employ two thousand and five hundred Marriners at least; and the building with the repayring of the sayd ships, here at home, will set to worke five hundred men, Carpenters, Cawkers, Carvers, Joyners, Smiths, & other laborers, besides many officers, and about 120. Factors, in severall places of the Indies. And so from these matters of great consequence, I must beginne to write of Beggery.

The fourth Part concernes the poverty of widdowes, &c.

The povertie of Widdowes and Fatherlesse is matter of great compassion, and doth alwaies move Christian hearts to commiseration and charitie; whereby many receive reliefe & helpe of those whom God hath blessed with better meanes: but how this poverty should totally be prevented, it seemeth not onely difficult, but altogether impossible: For besides the evill accidents and miseries, which ever attend on our humanity, we see how many dayly (even through their owne folly and wilfulnesse) do as it were desperately plunge themselves into adversitie. And thus the number of those is great, who having the charge of wife & children, are notwithstanding altogether without meanes and artes to procure their maintenance; whereby some of them, wanting grace, do run a desperate course, & have untimely ends. Others again, being better inspired, seek for imployment, but find it not, or with great difficulty: for, who doth willingly entertain a man poore and miserable, charged with

The East India Trade doth employ many poore men, & deboist people which other trades refuse.

a family, and peradventure debauched in conditions? Neither doe any of our other Merchants voyages to forraine parts accept of those novices who never have been used to the Sea: So that when all the other doores of charitie are shut, the East India gates stands wide open to receive the needy and the poore, giving them good entertainment, with two Moneths wages before hand, to make their neeedfull provisions for the voyage: And in the time of their absence, there is likewise payd unto their wives for maintenance, two other months wages upon accompt of every yeares service: and also if any chance to dye in the voyage, the Wife receiveth all that is found due unto her husband (if he do not otherwise dispose it by will:) and this often happeneth to be more money then ever they had of their owne together in any one time.

Wages before hand is not given in other Merchants voyages, neither yet so great wages as the East India company pay.

And likewise, are not many poore Widdowes, Wives, and Children of Blackewall, Lime-house, Ratcliffe, Shadwell, and Wapping, often relieved by the East India Company, with whole Hogsheads of good Biefe and Porke, Bisket, and doales of ready money? Are not divers of their children set on worke to pick Okam, & other labours fitting their age and capacitie? What might I not say of repayring of Churches, maintenance of some young Schollers, relieving of many poore Preachers of the Gospell yearely with good summes of money; and divers other acts of charitie, which are by them religiously

When did any of these widdowes beg for reliefe in our Churches, as others often doe?

The East India Company their charity.

performed, even in the times now of their worst fortunes? for all which I hope there shal be a reward unto them and theirs. And so I come to the fifth part of this third Objection.

The fifth Part concerneth the cheapnesse of Spice and Indico at this present in respect of former times.

And here I must intimate how much they are deceived who thinke that Spices and Indico are no better cheape in England now, then in times past, before the East India Trade began.

For, it is an undoubted truth, that in those dayes we often paid 6. shillings or more for a pound of Pepper, and seldome or never lesse then three shillings and sixe pence the pound; whereas since the Trade hath come directly from the Indies, it hath beene bought commonly at seuerall prices, betweene 16. pence and two shillings the pound; but I will make the difference of price appeare more plainely, by setting downe the quantities of Spices and Indico, which are yearely spent in the Realme of England, together with the lowest prices, which they were wont to sell at, when wee brought them from Turkey and Lixborne; and the like concerning their usuall prices now that wee bring them from the East Indies directly; And first as from Turkey.

Prices of Spice and Indico in former times.

lbs.	*l.*	*s.*	*d.*
400000 of Pepper at 3.s. 6.d. the pound.	*70000*	*00*	*00*
40000 of Cloves at 8.s. the pound.	*16000*	*00*	*00*
20000 of Maces at 9.s. the pound.	*9000*	*00*	*00*

lbs.	l.	s.	d.
5160000 of Nutmegs at 4.s. 6.d. the pound.	36000	00	00
150000 of Indico at 7.s. the pound.	52500	00	00
	183500	00	00

And the selfe same quantity and sorts of wares are commonly sold at the prices here under written now in these later times.

Prices of Spice and Indico in these latter times.

lbs.	l.	s.	d.
400000 of Pepper at 20.d. the pound.	33333	06	08
40000 of Cloves at 6.d. the pound.	12000	00	00
20000 of Maces at 6.s. the pound.	6000	00	00
160000 of Nutmegs at 2.s. 6.d. the pound.	20000	00	00
150000 of Indico at 5.s. the pound.	37000	00	00
	108333	06	08

Lesse than 18. thousand pounds sterling in the Indies, will buy Spice and Indico to serve this Realme for a yeare, which is not halfe so much money as it spendeth beyond the seas to buy Currans onely, or to buy Tobacco.

So that this Trade in Spice and Indico onely, doth save the Kingdome yearly 74966.l. 13.s. 04.d. which is a matter worthy to be observed; and so much the rather, because it is a certaine truth, that lesse than a quarter part of this sum of money which is thus saved yearely, shall buy in the Indies the full quantitie of all the severall sorts of wares before written, which doe serve for a yeares provision for this Realme of England; but still it must be remembered, that the custome, impost, wages, victuals, shipping, and other charges (which are to be added) will be a greater summe, then the mony which is paid for these wares in the Indies; but as I have noted before, the said charges doe not consume the Kingdomes stocke, although it doth greatly abate the Merchants gaine.

The wares only which are sent out of this kingdome into the East Indies are of sufficient value to furnish this Realme with an overplus of all manner of Indian wares (Persian Raw-Silkes only excepted.)

And to conclude this point, I will adde unto that which hath beene said; that the commodities onely which we now send yearely into the East Indies and Persia, are of sufficient value there, to returne us Indico, Spices, Drugs, and all other sorts of Indian wares, (Raw-silkes of Persia only excepted) for one yeares consume, or more in this Kingdome; So that now all the money which is sent forth in our Ships, doth procure an over-plus of the said wares to the furtherance of Trade from India hither, and after from hence to forreine parts againe, to the great imployment of the Subjects, and inriching of this Realme, both in Stocke and Treasure; all which is matter very worthy to be diligently observed; And so I come to give answer unto the fourth and last Objection.

IV

THE FOURTH OBJECTION.

IV

THE FOURTH OBJECTION.

It is generally observed that his Majesties Mint hath had but little imployment ever sithence the East India Trade began; wherefore it is manifest, that the onely remedie for this, and so many evils besides, is to put downe this Trade: For what other remedie can there be for the good of the Common-wealth?

THE ANSWER.

This fourth objection may be devided into three parts:

1. An evill declared.
2. A remedie propounded.
3. And counsell demaunded.

The first Part concerneth his Majesties Mint.

And first concerning the Evill or want of Silver, I thinke it hath beene, and is a generall disease of all Nations, and so will continue untill the end of the world; for poore and rich complaine they never have enough: but it seemeth the maladie is growen mortall here with us, and therefore it cries out for remedie: Well, I hope it is but imagination maketh us sicke, when all our parts be sound and strong; For who knoweth not the inestimable treasure of this Kingdome in Plate possessed by the people thereof almost of all degrees; in such measure, as neverhath beene seene in former ages?

25000 pounds waight at least of Silver yearely melted downe into Plate, besides old Plate new fashioned, as by credible report.

And for his Majesties Mint, it is well knowne, that there hath beene coyned in five yeares together since the East India Company began, 6214. pounds waight of Gold, and 311384. pound waight of sterling Money; all which Gold and Silver doe amount unto the summe of 1213850. pounds of sterling Money; How then doth this Trade turne the currant and imployment of the Mint?

There hath bin coyned great store of Gold and Silver in his Majesties Mint since the East India Trade began.

But upon the sight of this truth, perhaps it will be said, That wee must resort unto the present times, (the Mint being idle now.)

To which I answer, That likewise the Mint had little or no imployment for coynage of Silver in former times, when the said Company did not export above fifteene or twenty thousand pounds sterling at the most per annum; no, nor yet in the yeares 1608. and 1612: when in the former they shipped out but 6000.l. --00.s. --00.d. and in the latter, but 1250.l.--00.s.--00.d. sterling. So that both waies we see, that the Mint hath had

There hath bin little or no Silver coyned in some yeares, when the East India Company sent out very small sums of money.

very great imployment five yeares together, sithence the East India Trade began; and also it hath beene without imployment divers yeares, when the East India Company have sent away but very small summes of money; wherefore of necessitie there must be some other causes and meanes whereby our Silver is not exported onley, but also it is not imported into the Realme as in former times. For we have not had the meanes by our owne plentie, nor by the scarcitie of our neighbours, (for the space of the last foureteene yeares together) to send out hundreds of Ships laden with Corne, as in times past which was returned home in Silver; but rather of late yeares (as is much to be feared) a great quantitie of our money hath beene carried out of the Kingdome, for that Corne which hath beene brought us from the East Countries, and other places, to supply our wants. Thus times doe change, and our fortunes change with them: neither list I to make this matter plainer, by setting downe those meanes, which heretofore brought us store of money, even out of France and other places, which now are ceased. But without any further medling in the Mint, I will come to the remedie which some propound, by putting downe the East India Company.

Some causes and meanes which were wont to bring Silver into the Realme, are ceased at this present time.

But heere our comfort is, that the Obiectors are not our Judges, whose wisedome and integritie labouring for the honour of his Majestie, and the good of his Kingdome, will soon perceive the mischiefes of this supposed

The Second Part concerneth the putting downe of the East India Trade.

remedie. And that the pretended evill which many with malice chase, is that great good, which other Nations seeke by pollicie and strength to keepe, and likewise to obtaine; In which proceedings, it concerneth us, especially to observe the diligences and practices of the Dutch; who with more gladnesse would undertake the whole Trade to the East Indies, then with any reason we can abandon that part thereof, which we now enjoy; neither can our restraint from the Indies keepe our Silver from thence, as long as the Dutch goe thither: for we know, that devices want not to furnish such dessignes; and when their Ships returne from India, shall not our Silver out againe to helpe to pay a double price, or what they please, for all those wares which we shall want for our necessities?

The East India Trade is greatly desired by other Christian Nations.

The Dutch might grow strong and rich by our destruction.

Thus should the Dutch increase their honour, wealth and strength, whilest we abate, grow poore and weake at Sea for want of Trade; and call you this a Remedy; no, rather tearme it Ruine, Destruction, or what you list; And so I come unto the conclusion, or last part.

The Third Part concerneth the councel which the Objecters demand.

And here I must confesse my selfe aground, for this matter is much too high for my handling: besides, my excuse is faire, having already done my task to cleare the East India Trade from imputation; the which, for want of learning, although I have performed, without varietie of words or eloquence: yet it is done with all integritie of truth, in every particular, as I shall be readie to make proofe upon all occasions, which may bee offered. And yet before I make an end, although I cannot satisfie every mans desire, in such measure as is necessarie: yet I thinke it not amisse to performe the same so farre as I am able by common practise, and my observations in the Trade of Merchandize, which is my profession.

And first therefore, all men doe know, that the riches or sufficiencie of every Kingdome, State, or Common-wealth, consisteth in the possession of those things, which are needfull for a civill life.

The riches of a kingdome is of two sorts.

This sufficiency is of two sorts: the one is naturall, and proceedeth of the Territorie it selfe: the other is artificiall, and dependeth on the industry of the Inhabitants.

The Realme of England (praised be God) is happily possessed of them both: as first, having great plentie of naturall riches, both in the Sea for Fish, & on the Land for Wooll, Cattle, Corne, Lead, Tin, Iron, and many other things for Food, Rayment & Munition; insomuch, that upon strickt tearmes of need, this land may live without the help of any other Nation.

But to live well, to flourish and grow rich, we must finde meanes, by Trade to vent our superfluities; therewith to furnish and adorne us with the Treasure and those necessarie wares, which forreine Nations doe afford: and here industrie must begin to play

This kind of industry maketh some Countries which are poor

in themselves, to grow rich and strong by other Nations, who have greater meanes, and are lesse industrious.

his part, not onely to increase and guide the Trades abroad; but also to maintaine and multiply the Arts at home: for when either of these faile, or are not effected with such skill as their mysterie shall require, then doth the Common-wealth abate & growes poore; neither is this easily perceived at first, untill some evill accidents doe stir up our diligence to search out the true causes, that so they being removed, the effects may cease. And this is the subject of our discourse which we now pursue.

That which I have hitherto delivered, hath beene altogether Negative, still defending and proving by arguments, that the East India Trade hath not hurt this Common-wealth; and now changing my stile, I must affirme as fast the true causes of those evils which we seeke to chase away.

Foure Principall Causes which carry away our Gold and Silver.

These causes then (as I conceive) are principally foure.

1. The first is the breach of Entercourse by forraine Nations.

2. The second is the abuse of the exchanges betwixt us and other Countries.

3. The third is neglect of dutie in some Subiects.

4. The fourth is our dammage in Commerce with Strangers.

Now concerning all these, I might make a very large discourse; but my purpose is only to explane the meaning of every point in order, as briefely as I can.

And first for the breach of Entercourse; by this I understand those Nations, who have either debased their Standard, or else overvalued the price of their Coynes from that equivalence which formerly they had with the Standard and Moneys of this Realme; And also doe tollerate, not onely their owne Moneys, but also the Coyne of other Countries (and especially of this Kingdome) to bee currant with them at higher rates, then the prizes of the Exchange; by which courses (being directly against the Entercourse) there is a greater cause given of exportation of the Moneys of this Realme, then otherwise there would be. For although this is done with great danger to the exporters of the same, (it being an acte against the Law of the Land) yet notwithstanding Covetousnesse, being ever conversant in wicked actions, thinketh nothing unlawfull, which promiseth a certaine gaine; and how to remedie this evill practice, I finde it not easie. For the debasing of the Coyne, or raising the price thereof in this Realme, would much impoverish the estates of particular men, and yet in the conclusion, would prove a businesse without end: for who doth not conceive that which would follow beyond the Seas upon any such alteration here with us? so that still the evill will remaine,

The first Cause concerneth the Standard.

Proceedings against entercourse.

untill we find some other remedie.

The second Cause concerneth the Exchanges of moneys with forreine Countries.

And for the exchanges of money, used betwixt Nations, although the true use thereof is a very lawdable and necessarie practise, for the accommodating of Merchants affaires, and furnishing of Travellers in their occasions, without the transporting of Coyne from one State to another, with danger and losse, both to the publique and private wealth; yet is the abuse thereof verie prejudiciall unto this Kingdome in particuler; whilest in the interim the benefit doth arise unto other Countries, who diligently observing the prizes whereby the monies bee exchanged, may take advantage, to carrie away the Gold and Silver of this Realme at those times, when the rate of our sterling money (in Exchange) is under the value of that Standard, unto which place they are conveyed; For in respect the prizes of the Exchanges, doe rise and fall according to the plentie or scarcitie of money, which is to be taken up or delivered out, the exchange is hereby become rather a Trade for some great monyed men, then a furtherance and accomodation of reall Trade to Merchants, as it ought to be in the true use thereof.

The practise of those strangers here in this Realme, who make a Trade by Exchange of moneys.

And thus many times money may be made over hither by Strangers, to a good gaine, and presently carried beyond the Seas to a second profite, and yet the mischiefe ends not here: for by this means the takers up of money in forraine Countreys must necessarily drive a Trade to those places, from whence they draw their moneys; and so doe fill us up with forraine Commodities, without the vent of our owne wares, but for this great evill, there is an easie remedie, and so I come to handle the next cause which is neglect of Dutie.

Forraine wares brought in with our ready moneys carryed out of this Realme.

Neither is it my intent to write of Duties in their severall kindes; but onely of that kinde of duty which is here thought to bee neglected by some men in their severall vocations. As it might peradventure come to passe, in those who have the working of his Majesties coyne, either gold or silver: if diligent care be not had in the size of every severall peece, to answer justly to his weight: for howsoever upon triall of many peeces altogether, the weight may bee found according to the covenants, and within the remedies ordained in the Indentures: Yet notwithstanding many of those peeces may be sized too light, & others as much too heavy; which giveth the greater advantage to some people, to carry away that which is over-weight, and so to leave us them which are too light, if they leave us any.

The third cause concerneth neglect of duties.

Our heavy money is conveyed beyond the seas, and melted downe into plate here in the realme.

And this mischiefe is not single; for thereby also some Goldsmiths, regarding profit more then dutie, may bee the more readily drawne to melt downe the heavy Coyne into Plate and other ornaments both of gold and silver.

But what might wee thinke of those men who are placed in authoritie and office for his Majesty, if they should not with all

Anno 17. Edw. 4.

dutifull care discharge their trust concerning that excellent Statute, where in it is ordered, that all the moneys received by strangers for their Merchandize, shall be employed upon the commodities of this Realme? the due performance whereof would not onley prevent the carrying away of much gold and silver, but also be a meanes of greater vent of our owne wares: whereof I purpose to write something more in the next part which concerneth our commerce with strangers.

The fourth cause concerneth our commerce with strangers.

And now I come to the last point, which I feare is not the least amongst the causes of our want of money (so farre as any such may bee:) and let it not seeme strange to any man, that Trades should hurt and impoverish a Commonwealth, since it hath beene alwayes accompted an excellent means to helpe and enrich the same: for, as this truth cannot be denyed with reason, so it is likewise most certain, that the unskilfull managing thereof hath ever prooved a great decay unto those Nations who have been entangled with such errors. And are not the examples too frequent in many of our owne Merchants, who not onely by the perils of the Seas and such like misfortunes, lose their goods, but also even through want of knowledge, wisely to direct their affaires, doe overthrow their whole estates: neither may we properly call this their losse, but rather the Kingdomes losse in them. Wherefore it were to be wished, that this mysterie of Merchandizing might

Unskilfull Merchants overthrow our Trades.

be left only to them, who have had education thereunto; and not to be undertaken by such, who leaving their proper vocations, doe for want of skill in this, both overthrow themselves & others who are better practised. But there is yet a farre greater mischiefe by our Trades beyond the Seas, when peradventure, there might be imported yearely a greater value in forraine wares, then by any way or meanes we doe export of our owne commodities; which cannot otherwise come to passe, then with a manifest impoverishing of the Commonwealth; for as it is a certaine cause to make us rich, both in stock & treasure, when we shall carry out a greater value of our owne goods then we bring in of forraine wares; so by consequence, a course contrary to this, must of necessity worke a contrary effect.

Merchants by education are onely fit to trade in forren parts.

How rich Commonwealths may become poore.

Neither is this importation meant otherwise the concerning those wares, which are consumed in this Realm: for the commodities which are brought in & after carried out unto forren parts again, cannot hurt, but doe greatly help the Commonwealth, by encrease of his Majesties Customes and Trades, with other imployments of the subiects; by which particulars I might yet set foorth the glory of the East India Trade, which hath brought into this Realme in fifteene moneths space, not onley so much Spice, as hath served the same for the sayd time; but also by the superfluitie thereof, there hath beene exported into forraine parts for about 215000. pounds

Forraine wares brought in for Transito, cannot hurt, but greatly helpe the Commonwealth.

Hopes to encrease Trade by exportation of Indian wares to forrain parts.

sterling. So then let all men judge, for what a great value wee may hope hereafter to export yearely: when unto these spices we may (by Gods assistance) add the infinite worth of Raw-silkes, Indicos, Callicoes, and some other things: All which are to bee issued in the nature of Cloth, Lead, Tinne, or any of our owne Merchandize to the enriching of this Kingdome by encrease of the Common-stocke. So then to conclude this poynt, we ought not to avoid the importation of forraine wares, but rather willingly to bridle our owne affections to the moderate consuming of the same: for otherwise, howsoever the East India Trade in particular is an excellent meanes greatly to encrease the stocke of mony which we send thither yearely, by returning home five times the value thereof in rich commodities, all which (in short time) may bee converted into Treasure, as is plainly shewd already in Page 47. Yet notwithstanding, if these Indian wares thus brought home, cannot be spared to serve for that purpose of Treasure; but must be sent forth together with our owne native commodities: and yet all little enough to provide our excesse and extraordinary consume of forraine wares: then is it likewise as certaine that the generall Trade of this Kingdome doth hinder and divert the comming in of the said Treasure, by over-ballancing the value of our wares exported; with the importation and immoderate consume of forraine Commodities.

The particular Trade to the East Indies wil bring great store of treasure into this Realme, if the generall Trade of this Kingdome doe not hinder and consume it.

Therefore, forasmuch as the number of the people in this Realme, are thought to be greatly increased of late time (both in themselves and strangers) whereby necessarily the Commodities of this Kingdome, and also forraine wares, are the more consumed and wasted (a double meanes to abate the Common-wealth;) it therefore concerneth us all in generall, and every man in his particular, to stirre up our minds, and diligence, to helpe the naturall Commodities of this Realme by industrie, and increase of Arts; seeing that the materials cannot bee wanting to make such Stuffes, and other things as are daily brought unto us from forraine parts, to the great advantage of Strangers, and to our no lesse dammage. Neither should we neglect the riches which our Seas affoord, whilest other Nations by their labour doe procure themselves great Treasure from the same. And as the diligent performance of these things, would plentifully maintaine the poore, and much increase the common stocke of this Kingdome: so likewise for the better furtherance thereof, wee ought religiously to avoid our common excesses of food and rayment, which is growne to such a height in most degrees of people (above their abilitie) that it is now beyond all example of former ages. Neither is it needfull for me, to set downe the particulars of these abuses; for they are too well knowne: and I am confident, that the wisedome of our Government doth endevour to see them as well amended, to the

The Dutch in particular, are said to reape such infinite wealth yearely by this fishing Trade, that without more certain knowledge thereof I dare not set down the sum, it seemeth so uncredible.

glorie of God, the honour of the King, and the good of the Common-wealth.

Amen.

FINIS.

ENGLAND's
TREASURE
BY
Forraign Trade.
OR,
The Ballance of our Forraign Trade
IS
The Rule of our Treasure.

Written by THOMAS MUN, *of* Lond. *Merchant*,

And now published for the Common good by his Son JOHN MUN *of* Bearsted *in the County of* Kent, *Esquire.*

LONDON,

Printed by *J. G.* for *Thomas Clark*, and are to be sold at his Shop at the South entrance of the *Royal Exchange.* 1664.

TO THE RIGHT HONOURABLE,

THOMAS

EARL OF

SOUTH-HAMPTON

LORD HIGH TREASURER OF ENGLAND,
LORD WARDEN OF THE NEW FORREST,
KNIGHT OF THE MOST NOBLE ORDER OF
THE GARTER, AND ONE OF HIS MAJESTY'S
MOST HONOURABLE PRIVY COUNCIL.

TO THE RIGHT HONOURABLE,

THOMAS

EARL OF

SOUTH-HAMPTON

Lord High Treasurer of England, Lord Warden of the New Forrest, Knight of the most Noble Order of the Garter, and one of His Majesty's most Honourable Privy Council.

My Lord,

I Present this ensuing Treatise to your Lordship as its proper Patron, to whom, by vertue of your great Trust (the greatest, doubtless, in this Kingdome) the management of his Majesty's Treasure, and improvement of his Revenue, are most peculiarly committed.

The title of it (Englands Treasure by Forraign Trade) alone bespeaks your notice, the Argument, (being of so publick a nature) may invite your perusall but the Tract it self will, I hope, deserve your Lordships Protection. It was left me in the nature of a Legacy by my Father, for whose sake I cannot but value it as one of my best Moveables, and as such I dedicate it to your Lordship.

He was in his time famous amongst Merchants, and well known to most men of business, for his general Experience in Affairs, and notable Insight into Trade; neither was he less observed for his Integrity to his Prince, and Zeal to the Common-wealth: the serious Discourses of such men are commonly not unprofitable.

To your Lordships judgement I submit this Treatise, and my presumption herein to your Pardon.

My Lord,

Your most faithful and
obedient Servant,

John Mun.

ENGLAND'S TREASURE
BY
FORRAIGN TRADE
OR,
THE BALLANCE OF OUR FORRAIGN TRADE IS THE RULE OF OUR TREASURE.

ENGLAND'S TREASURE BY FORRAIGN TRADE OR, THE BALLANCE OF OUR FORRAIGN TRADE IS THE RULE OF OUR TREASURE.

My Son, In a former Discourse I have endeavoured after my manner briefly to teach thee two things: The first is Piety, how to fear God aright, according to his Works and Word: The second is Policy, how to love and serve thy Country, by instructing thee in the duties and proceedings of sundry Vocations, which either order, or else act the affairs of the Common-wealth; In which, as some things doe especially tend to Preserve, and others are more apt to Enlarge the same: So am I now to speak of Money, which doth indifferently serve to both those happy ends. Wherein I will observe this order, First, to shew the general means whereby a Kingdome may be enriched; and then proceed to those particular courses by which Princes are accustomed to be supplyed with Treasure. But first of all I will say something of the Merchant, because he must be a Principal Agent in this great business.

I

THE QUALITIES WHICH ARE REQUIRED IN A PERFECT MERCHANT OF FORRAIGN TRADE.

I

THE QUALITIES WHICH ARE REQUIRED IN A PERFECT MERCHANT OF FORRAIGN TRADE.

The love and service of our Country consisteth not so much in the knowledge of those duties which are to be performed by others, as in the skilful practice of that which is done by our selves; and therefore (my Son) it is now fit that I say something of the Merchant, which I hope in due time shall be thy Vocation. Yet herein are my thoughts free from all Ambition, although I rank thee in a place of so high estimation; for the Merchant is worthily called The Steward of the Kingdoms Stock, by way of Commerce with other Nations; a work of no less Reputation than Trust, which ought to be performed with great skill and conscience, that so the private gain may ever accompany the publique good. And because the nobleness of this Profession may the better stir up thy desires and endeavours to obtain those abilities which may effect it worthily,

As it is very commendable to know what is to be done by others in their places: So it were a great shame to be ignorant in the duties of our own Vocations.

I will briefly set down the excellent qualities which are required in a perfect Merchant.

1. He ought to be a good Penman, a good Arithmetician, and a good Accomptant, by that noble order of Debtor and Creditor, which is used onely amongst Merchants; also to be expert in the order and form of Charter-parties, Bills of Lading, Invoyces, Contracts, Bills of Exchange, and Policies of Ensurance.

2. He ought to know the Measures, Weights, and Monies of all forraign Countries, especially where we have Trade, & the Monies not onely by their several denominations, but also by their intrinsique values in weight & fineness, compared with the Standard of this Kingdome, without which he cannot well direct his affaires.

3. He ought to know the Customs, Tolls, Taxes, Impositions, Conducts, and other charges upon all manner of Merchandize exported or imported to and from the said Forraign Countries.

4. He ought to know in what several commodities each Country abounds, and what be the wares which they want, and how and from whence they are furnished with the same.

5. He ought to understand and to be a

diligent observer of the rates of Exchanges by Bills, from one State to another, whereby he may the better direct his affairs, and remit over and receive home his Monies to the most advantage possible.

6. He ought to know what goods are prohibited to be exported or imported in the said forraign Countreys, lest otherwise he should incur great danger and loss in the ordering of his affairs.

7. He ought to know upon what rates and conditions to fraight his Ships, and ensure his adventures from one Countrey to another, and to be well acquainted with the laws, orders and customes of the Ensurance office both here and beyond the Seas, in the many accidents which may happen upon the damage or loss of Ships or goods, or both these.

8. He ought to have knowledge in the goodness and in the prices of all the several materials which are required for the building and repairing of Ships, and the divers workmanships of the same, as also for the Masts, Tackling, Cordage, Ordnance, Victuals, Munition and Provisions of many kinds; together with the ordinary wages of Commanders, Officers and Mariners, all which concern the Merchant as he is an Owner of Ships.

9. He ought (by the divers occasions which happen sometime in the buying and selling of one commodity and sometimes in another) to have indifferent if not perfect knowledge in all manner of Merchandize or wares, which is to be as it were a man of all occupations and trades.

10. He ought by his voyaging on the Seas to become skilful in the Art of Navigation.

11. He ought as he is a Traveller, and sometimes abiding in forraign Countreys to attain to the speaking of divers Languages, and to be a diligent observer of the ordinary Revenues and expences of forraign Princes, together with their strength both by Sea and Land, their laws, customes, policies, manners, religions, arts, and the like; to be able to give account thereof in all occasions for the good of his Countrey.

12. Lastly, although there be no necessity that such a Merchant should be a great Scholar; yet is it (at least) required, that in his youth he learn the Latine tongue, which will the better enable him in all the rest of his endeavours.

Thus have I briefly shewed thee a pattern for thy diligence, the Merchant in his qualities; which in truth are such and so many, that I find no other profession that leadeth into more worldly knowledge. And it cannot be denied but that their sufficiency doth appear likewise in the excellent government of State at Venice, Luca, Genoua, Florence, the low Countreys, and divers other places of Christendom. And in those States also where they are least esteemed, yet is their skill and knowledge often used by those who sit in the highest places of Authority: It is therefore an act beyond rashness in some, who do disenable their Counsel and judgment (even in books printed) making them uncapable of those ways and means which do either enrich or empoverish a Common-wealth, when in truth this is only effected by the mystery of their trade, as I shall plainly shew in that which followeth. It is true indeed that many merchants here in England find less encouragement given to their profession than in other Countreys, and seeing themselves not so well esteemed as their Noble Vocation requireth, and according to the great consequence of the same, doe not therefore labour to attain unto the excellencie of their profession, neither is it practised by the Nobility of this Kingdom as it is in other States from the Father to the Son throughout their generations, to the great encrease of their wealth, and maintenance of their names and families: Whereas the memory of our richest Merchants is suddenly extinguished; the Son being left rich, scorneth the profession of his Father, conceiving more honour to

There is more honour and profit in an Industrious life, than in a great Inheritance which wasteth for want of vertue.

be a Gentleman (although but in name) to consume his estate in dark ignorance and excess, than to follow the steps of his Father as an Industrious Merchant to maintain and advance his Fortunes. But now leaving the Merchants praise we will come to his practice, or at least to so much thereof as concerns the bringing of Treasure into the Kingdom.

II

THE MEANS TO ENRICH THE KINGDOM, AND TO ENCREASE OUR TREASURE.

II

THE MEANS TO ENRICH THE KINGDOM, AND TO ENCREASE OUR TREASURE.

Although a Kingdom may be enriched by gifts received, or by purchase taken, from some other Nations, yet these are things uncertain and of small consideration when they happen. The ordinary means therefore to encrease our wealth and treasure is by Forraign Trade, wherein wee must ever observe this rule; to sell more to strangers yearly than wee consume of theirs in value. For suppose that when this Kingdom is plentifully served with the Cloth, Lead, Tinn, Iron, Fish and other native commodities, we doe yearly export the overplus to forraign Countries to the value of twenty two hundred thousand pounds; by which means we are enabled beyond the Seas to buy and bring in forraign wares for our use and Consumptions, to the value of twenty hundred thousand pounds; By this order duly kept in our trading, we may rest assured that

Forraign Trade is the Rule of our Treasure.

the Kingdom shall be enriched yearly two hundred thousand pounds, which must be brought to us in so much Treasure; because that part of our stock which is not returned to us in wares must necessarily be brought home in treasure.

For in this case it cometh to pass in the stock of a Kingdom, as in the estate of a private man; who is supposed to have one thousand pounds yearly revenue and two thousand pounds of ready money in his Chest: If such a man through excess shall spend one thousand five hundred pounds per annum, all his ready mony will be gone in four years; and in the like time his said money will be doubled if he take a Frugal course to spend but five hundred pounds per annum; which rule never faileth likewise in the Commonwealth, but in some cases (of no great moment) which I will hereafter declare, when I shall shew by whom and in what manner this ballance of the Kingdom's account ought to be drawn up yearly, or so often as it shall please the State to discover how much we gain or lose by trade with forraign Nations. But first I will say something concerning those ways and means which will encrease our exportations and diminish our importations of wares; which being done, I will then set down some other arguments both affirmative and negative to strengthen that which is here declared, and thereby to shew that all the other means which are commonly supposed to enrich the Kingdom with Treasure are altogether insufficient and meer fallacies.

III

THE PARTICULAR WAYS AND MEANS TO ENCREASE THE EXPORTATION OF OUR COMMODITIES, AND TO DECREASE OUR CONSUMPTION OF FORRAIGN WARES.

III

THE PARTICULAR WAYS AND MEANS TO ENCREASE THE EXPORTATION OF OUR COMMODITIES, AND TO DECREASE OUR CONSUMPTION OF FORRAIGN WARES.

The revenue or stock of a Kingdom by which it is provided of forraign wares is either Natural or Artificial. The Natural wealth is so much only as can be spared from our own use and necessities to be exported unto strangers. The Artificial consists in our manufactures and industrious trading with forraign commodities, concerning which I will set down such particulars as may serve for the cause we have in hand.

1. First, although this Realm be already exceeding rich by nature, yet might it be much encreased by laying the waste grounds (which are infinite) into such employments as should no way hinder the present revenues of

other manured lands, but hereby to supply our selves and prevent the importations of Hemp, Flax, Cordage, Tobacco, and divers other things which now we fetch from strangers to our great impoverishing.

2. We may likewise diminish our importations, if we would soberly refrain from excessive consumption of forraign wares in our diet and rayment, with such often change of fashions as is used, so much the more to encrease the waste and charge; which vices at this present are more notorious amongst us than in former ages. Yet might they easily be amended by enforcing the observation of such good laws as are strictly practised in other Countries against the said excesses; where likewise by commanding their own manufactures to be used, they prevent the coming in of others, without prohibition, or offence to strangers in their mutual commerce.

3. In our exportations we must not only regard our own superfluities, but also we must consider our neighbours necessities, that so upon the wares which they cannot want, nor yet be furnished thereof elsewhere, we may (besides the vent of the Materials) gain so much of manifacture as we can, and also endeavour to sell them dear, so far forth as the high price cause not a less vent in the quantity. But the superfluity of our commodities which strangers use, and may also have the same

from other Nations, or may abate their vent by the use of some such like wares from other places, and with little inconvenience; we must in this case strive to sell as cheap as possible we can, rather than to lose the utterance of such wares. For we have found of late years by good experience, that being able to sell our Cloth cheap in Turkey, we have greatly encreased the vent thereof, and the Venetians have lost as much in the utterance of theirs in those Countreys, because it is dearer. And on the other side a few years past, when by the excessive price of Wools our Cloth was exceeding dear, we lost at the least half our clothing for forraign parts, which since is no otherwise (well neer) recovered again than by the great fall of price for Wools and Cloth. We find that twenty five in the Hundred less in the price of these and some other Wares, to the loss of private mens revenues, may raise above fifty upon the hundred in the quantity vented to the benefit of the publique. For when Cloth is dear, other Nations doe presently practise clothing, and we know they want neither art nor materials to this performance. But when by cheapness we drive them from this employment, and so in time obtain our dear price again, then do they also use their former remedy. So that by these alterations we learn, that it is in vain to expect a greater revenue of our wares than their condition will afford, but rather it concerns us to apply our endeavours to the times with care and diligence to help

The State in some occasions may gain most, when private men by their revenues get least.

our selves the best we may, by making our cloth and other manufactures without deceit, which will encrease their estimation and use.

4. The value of our exportations likewise may be much advanced when we perform it ourselves in our own Ships, for then we get only not the price of our wares as they are worth here, but also the Merchants gains, the charges of ensurance, and fraight to carry them beyond the seas. As for example, if the Italian Merchants should come hither in their own shipping to fetch our Corn, our red Herrings or the like, in this case the Kingdom should have ordinarily but 25. s. for a quarter of Wheat, and 20. s. for a barrel of red herrings, whereas if we carry these wares ourselves into Italy upon the said rates, it is likely that wee shall obtain fifty shillings for the first, and forty shillings for the last, which is a great difference in the utterance or vent of the Kingdoms stock. And, although it is true that the commerce ought to be free to strangers to bring in and carry out at their pleasure, yet nevertheless in many places the exportation of victuals and munition are either prohibited, or at least limited to be done onely by the people and Shipping of those places where they abound.

5. The frugal expending likewise of our own natural wealth might advance much yearly to be exported unto strangers; and if

in our rayment we will be prodigal, yet let this be done with our own materials and manufactures, as Cloth, Lace, Imbroderies, Cutworks and the like, where the excess of the rich may be the employment of the poor, whose labours notwithstanding of this kind, would be more profitable for the Commonwealth, if they were done to the use of Strangers.

6. The Fishing in his Majesties seas of England, Scotland and Ireland is our natural wealth, and would cost nothing but labour, which the Dutch bestow willingly, and thereby draw yearly a very great profit to themselves by serving many places of Christendom with our Fish, for which they return and supply their wants both of forraign Wares and Mony, besides the multitudes of Mariners and Shipping, which hereby are maintain'd, whereof a long discourse might be made to shew the particular manage of this important business. Our Fishing plantation likewise in New-England, Virginia, Groenland, the Summer Islands and the New-found-land, are of the like nature, affording much wealth and employments to maintain a great number of poor, and to encrease our decaying trade.

How some States have been made Rich.

7. A Staple or Magazin for forraign Corn, Indico, Spices, Raw-silks, Cotton wool or any other commodity whatsoever, to be imported will encrease Shipping, Trade, Treasure, and the Kings customes, by exporting them again

where need shall require, which course of Trading, hath been the chief means to raise Venice, Genoa, the low-Countreys, with some others; and for such a purpose England stands most commodiously, wanting nothing to this performance but our own diligence and endeavour.

8. Also wee ought to esteem and cherish those trades which we have in remote or far Countreys, for besides the encrease of Shipping and Mariners thereby, the wares also sent thither and received from thence are far more profitable unto the kingdom than by our trades neer at hand; As for example; suppose Pepper to be worth here two Shillings the pound constantly, if then it be brought from the Dutch at Amsterdam, the Merchant may give there twenty pence the pound, and gain well by the bargain, but if he fetch this Pepper from the East-indies, he must not give above three pence the pound at the most, which is a mighty advantage, not only in that part which serveth for our own use, but also for that great quantity which (from hence) we transport yearly unto divers other Nations to be sold at a higher price: whereby it is plain, that we make a far greater stock by gain upon these Indian Commodities, than those Nations doe where they grow, and to whom they properly appertain, being the natural wealth of their Countries. But for the better understanding of this particular, we

The traffick in the East Indies is our most profitable trade in its proportion both for King and Kingdom.

We get more by the Indian wares than the Indians themselves.

must ever distinguish between the gain of the Kingdom, and the profit of the Merchant; for although the Kingdom payeth no more for this Pepper than is before supposed, nor for any other commodity bought in forraign parts more than the Stranger receiveth from us for the same, yet the Merchant payeth not only that price, but also the fraight, ensurance, customes and other charges which are exceeding great in these long voyages; but yet all these in the Kingdoms accompt are but commutations among our selves, and no privation of the Kingdoms stock, which being duly considered, together with the support also of our other trades in our best Shipping to Italy, France, Turkey, the East Countreys and other places, by transporting and venting the wares which we bring yearly from the East Indies; It may well stir up our utmost endeavours to maintain and enlarge this great and noble business, so much importing the Publique wealth, Strength, and Happiness. Neither is there less honour and judgment by growing rich (in this manner) upon the stock of other Nations, than by an industrious encrease of our own means, especially when this later is advanced by the benefit of the former, as we have found in the East Indies by sale of much of our Tin, Cloth, Lead and other Commodities, the vent whereof doth daily encrease in those Countreys which formerly had no use of our wares.

A distinction between the Kingdoms gain and the Merchants profit.

9. It would be very beneficial to export money as well as wares, being done in trade only, it would encrease our Treasure; but of this I write more largely in the next Chapter to prove it plainly.

10. It were policie and profit for the State to suffer manufactures made of forraign Materials to be exposed custome-free, as Velvets and all other wrought Silks, Fustians, thrown Silks and the like, it would employ very many poor people, and much encrease the value of our stock yearly issued into other Countreys, and it would (for this purpose) cause the more forraign Materials to be brought in, to the improvement of His Majesties Customes. I will here remember a notable increase in our manufacture of winding and twisting only of forraign raw Silk, which within 35. years to my knowledge did not employ more than 300. people in the City and suburbs of London, where at this present time it doth set on work above fourteen thousand souls, as upon diligent enquiry hath been credibly reported unto His Majesties Commissioners for Trade. And it is certain, that if the said forraign Commodities might be exported from hence, free of custome, this manufacture would yet encrease very much, and decrease as fast in Italy and the Netherlands. But if any man allege the Dutch proverb, Live and let others live; I answer, that the Dutchmen notwithstanding their own Proverb, doe not

onely in these Kingdoms, encroach upon our livings, but also in other forraign parts of our trade (where they have power) they do hinder and destroy us in our lawful course of living, hereby taking the bread out of our mouth, which we shall never prevent by plucking the pot from their nose, as of late years too many of us do practise to the great hurt and dishonour of this famous Nation; We ought rather to imitate former times in taking sober and worthy courses more pleasing to God and suitable to our ancient reputation.

11. It is needful also not to charge the native commodities with too great customes, lest by indearing them to the strangers use, it hinder their vent. And especially forraign wares brought in to be transported again should be favoured, for otherwise that manner of trading (so much importing the good of the Common wealth) cannot prosper nor subsist. But the Consumption of such forraign wares in the Realm may be the more charged, which will turn to the profit of the Kingdom in the Ballance of the Trade, and thereby also enable the King to lay up the more Treasure out of his yearly incomes, as of this particular I intend to write more fully in his proper place, where I shall shew how much money a Prince may conveniently lay up without the hurt of his subjects.

12. Lastly, in all things we must endeavour

to make the most we can of our own, whether it be Natural or Artificial; And forasmuch as the people which live by the Arts are far more in number than they who are masters of the fruits, we ought the more carefully to maintain those endeavours of the multitude, in whom doth consist the greatest strength and riches both of King and Kingdom: for where the people are many, and the arts good, there the traffique must be great, and the Countrey rich. The Italians employ a greater number of people, and get more money by their industry and manufactures of the raw Silks of the Kingdom of Cicilia, than the King of Spain and his Subjects have by the revenue of this rich commodity. But what need we fetch the example so far, when we know that our own natural wares doe not yield us so much profit as our industry? For Iron oar in the Mines is of no great worth, when it is compared with the employment and advantage it yields being digged, tried, transported, bought, sold, cast into Ordnance, Muskets, and many other instruments of war for offence and defence, wrought into Anchors, bolts, spikes, nayles and the like, for the use of Ships, Houses, Carts, Coaches, Ploughs, and other instruments for Tillage. Compare our Fleece-wools with our Cloth, which requires shearing, washing, carding, spinning, Weaving, fulling, dying, dressing and other trimmings, and we shall find these Arts more profitable than the natural wealth, whereof I might instance other examples, but I will not be more tedious, for if I would amplify upon this and the other particulars before written, I might find matter sufficient to make a large volume, but my desire in all is only to prove what I propound with brevity and plainness.

IV

THE EXPORTATION OF OUR MONEYS IN TRADE OF MERCHANDIZE IS A MEANS TO ENCREASE OUR TREASURE.

IV

THE EXPORTATION OF OUR MONEYS IN TRADE OF MERCHANDIZE IS A MEANS TO ENCREASE OUR TREASURE.

This Position is so contrary to the common opinion, that it will require many and strong arguments to prove it before it can be accepted of the Multitude, who bitterly exclaim when they see any monies carried out of the Realm; affirming thereupon that we have absolutely lost so much Treasure, and that this is an act directly against the long continued laws made and confirmed by the wisdom of this Kingdom in the High Court of Parliament, and that many places, nay Spain it self which is the Fountain of Mony, forbids the exportation thereof, some cases only excepted. To all which I might answer that Venice, Florence, Genoa, the Low Countreys and divers other places permit it, their people applaud it, and find great benefit by it; but all this makes a noise and proves nothing, we must therefore come to those reasons which concern the business in question.

First, I will take that for granted which no man of judgment will deny, that we have no other means to get Treasure but by forraign trade, for Mines wee have none which do afford it, and how this mony is gotten in the managing of our said Trade I have already shewed, that it is done by making our commodities which are exported yearly to over ballance in value the forraign wares which we consume; so that it resteth only to shew how our monyes may be added to our commodities, and being jointly exported may so much the more encrease our Treasure.

Wee have already supposed our yearly consumptions of forraign wares to be for the value of twenty hundred thousand pounds, and our exportations to exceed that two hundred thousand pounds, which sum wee have thereupon affirmed is brought to us in treasure to ballance the accompt. But now if we add three hundred thousand pounds more in ready mony unto our former exportations in wares, what profit can we have (will some men say) although by this means we should bring in so much ready mony more than wee did before, seeing that we have carried out the like value.

To this the answer is, that when wee have prepared our exportations of wares, and sent out as much of everything as wee can spare or vent abroad: It is not therefore said

Money begets trade and trade encreaseth mony.

that then We should add our money thereunto to fetch in the more mony immediately, but rather first to enlarge our trade by enabling us to bring in more forraign wares, which being sent out again will in due time much encrease our Treasure.

For although in this manner wee do yearly multiply our importations to the maintenance of more Shipping and Mariners, improvement of His Majesties Customs and other benefits: yet our consumption of those forraign wares is no more than it was before; so that all the said encrease of commodities brought in by the means of our ready mony sent out as is afore written, doth in the end become an exportation unto us of far greater value than our said moneys were, which is proved by three several examples following.

1. For I suppose that 100000. l. being sent in our Shipping to the East Countreys, will buy there one hundred thousand quarters of wheat cleer abroad the Ships, which after being brought into England and housed, to export the same at the best time for vent thereof in Spain or Italy, it cannot yield less in those parts than two hundred thousand pounds to make the Merchant but a saver, yet by this reckning we see the Kingdom hath doubled that Treasure.

2. Again this profit will be far greater when wee trade thus in remote Countreys,

as for example, if wee send one hundred thousand pounds into the East-Indies to buy Pepper there, and bring it hither, and from hence send it for Italy or Turkey, it must yield seven hundred thousand pounds at least in those places, in regard of the excessive charge which the Merchant disburseth in those long voyages in Shipping, Wages, Victuals, Insurance, Interest, Customes, Imposts, and the like, all which notwithstanding the King and the Kingdom gets.

Remote trades are most gainful to the Commonwealth.

3. But where the voyages are short & the wares rich, which therefore will not employ much Shipping, the profit will be far less. As when another hundred thousand pounds shall be employed in Turkey in raw Silks, and brought hither to be after transported from hence into France, the Low Countreys, or Germany, the Merchant shall have good gain, although he sell it there but for one hundred and fifty thousand pounds: and thus take the voyages altogether in their Medium, the moneys exported will be returned unto us more than Trebled. But if any man will yet object, that these returns come to us in wares, and not really in mony as they were issued out,

The answer is (keeping our first ground) that if our consumption of forraign wares be no more yearly than is already supposed, and that our exportations be so mightily encreased by this manner of Trading with ready money as is before declared: it is not then possible but that all the over-ballance or difference should return either in mony or in such wares as we must export again, which, as is already plainly shewed will be still a greater means to encrease our Treasure.

For it is in the stock of the Kingdom as in the estates of private men, who having store of wares, doe not therefore say that they will not venture out or trade with their mony (for this were ridiculous) but do also turn that into wares, whereby they multiply their Mony, and so by a continual and orderly change of one into the other grow rich, and when they please turn all their estates into Treasure; for they that have Wares cannot want mony.

The proverb saith, He that hath ware hath mony by the year.

Neither is it said that Mony is the Life of Trade, as if it could not subsist without the same; for we know that there was great trading by way of commutation or barter when there was little mony stirring in the world. The Italians and some other Nations have such remedies against this want, that it can neither decay nor hinder their trade, for they transfer bills of debt, and have Banks both publick and private, wherein they do assign their credits from one to another daily for very great sums with ease and satisfaction by writings only, whilst in the mean time the Mass of Treasure which gave foundation to these credits is employed in Forraign Trade as a Merchandize, and by the said means they have little other use of money in those countreys more than for their ordinary expences. It is not therefore the keeping of our mony in the Kingdom, but the necessity and use of our wares in forraign Countries, and our want of their commodities that causeth the vent and consumption on all sides, which makes a quick and ample Trade. If wee were once poor, and now having gained some store of mony by trade with resolution to keep it still in the Realm; shall this cause other Nations to spend more of our commodities than formerly they have done, whereby we might say that our trade is Quickned and Enlarged? no verily it will produce no such good effect: but rather according to the alteration of times by their true causes wee may expect the contrary; for all men do consent that plenty of mony in a Kingdom doth make the native commodities dearer, which as it is to the profit of some private men in their revenues, so is it directly against the benefit of the Publique in the quantity of the trade; for as plenty of mony makes wares dearer, so dear wares decline their use and consumption, as hath been already plainly shewed in the last Chapter upon that particular of our cloth; And although this is a very hard lesson for some great landed men to learn, yet I am sure it is a true lesson for all the land to observe, lest when wee have gained some store of mony by trade, wee lose it again by not trading with our mony. I knew a Prince in Italy (of famous memory) Ferdinando the first, great

Duke of Tuscanie, who being very rich in Treasure, endevoured therewith to enlarge his trade by issuing out to his Merchants great sums of money for very small profit; I my self had forty thousand crowns of him gratis for a whole year, although he knew that I would presently send it away in Specie for the parts of Turkey to be employed in wares for his Countries, he being well assured that in this course of trade it would return again (according to the old saying) with a Duck in the mouth. This noble and industrious Prince by his care and diligence to countenance and favour Merchants in their affairs, did so encrease the practice thereof, that there is scarce a Nobleman or Gentleman in all his dominions that doth not Merchandize either by himself or in partnership with others, whereby within these thirty years the trade to his port of Leghorn is so much encreased, that of a poor little town (as I my self knew it) it is now become a fair and strong City, being one of the most famous places for trade in all Christendom. And yet it is worthy our observation, that the multitude of Ships and wares which come hither from England, the Low Countreys, and other places, have little or no means to make their returns from thence but only in ready mony, which they may and do carry away freely at all times, to the incredible advantage of the said great Duke of Tuscanie and his subjects, who are much enriched by the continual great concourse of

Merchants from all the States of the neighbour Princes, bringing them plenty of mony daily to supply their wants of the said wares. And thus we see that the current of Merchandize which carries away their Treasure, becomes a flowing stream to fill them again in a greater measure with mony.

There is yet an objection or two as weak as all the rest: that is, if wee trade with our Mony wee shall issue out the less wares; as if a man should say, those Countreys which heretofore had occasion to consume our Cloth, Lead, Tin, Iron, Fish, and the like, shall now make use of our monies in the place of these necessaries, which were most absurd to affirm, or that the Merchant had not rather carry out wares by which there is ever some gains expected, than to export mony which is still but the same without any encrease.

But on the contrary there are many Countreys which may yield us very profitable trade for our mony, which otherwise afford us no trade at all, because they have no use of our wares, as namely the East-Indies for one in the first beginning thereof, although since by industry in our commerce with those Nations we have brought them into the use of much of our Lead, Cloth, Tin, and other things, which is a good addition to the former vent of our commodities.

Again, some men have alleged that those Countries which permit mony to be carried out, do it because they have few or no wares to trade withall: but wee have great store of commodities, and therefore their action ought not to be our example.

To this the answer is briefly, that if we have such a quantity of wares as doth fully provide us of all things needful from beyond the seas: why should we then doubt that our monys sent out in trade, must not necessarily come back again in treasure; together with the great gains which it may procure in such manner as is before set down? And on the other side, if those Nations which send out their monies do it because they have but few wares of their own, how come they then to have so much Treasure as we ever see in those places which suffer it freely to be exported at all times and by whomsoever? I answer, Even by trading with their Moneys; for by what other means can they get it, having no Mines of Gold or Sliver?

Our humane actions ought especially to be considered in their ends.

Thus may we plainly, see, that when this weighty business is duly considered in his end, as all our humane actions ought well to be weighed, it is found much contrary to that which most men esteem thereof, because they search no further than the beginning of the work, which mis-informs their judgments, and leads them into error: For if we only behold the actions of the husbandman in the seed-time when he casteth away much good corn into the ground, we will rather accompt him a mad man than a husbandman: but when we consider his labours in the harvest which is the end of his endeavours, we find the worth and plentiful encrease of his actions.

V

FORRAIGN TRADE IS THE ONLY MEANS TO IMPROVE THE PRICE OF OUR LANDS.

V

FORRAIGN TRADE IS THE ONLY MEANS TO IMPROVE THE PRICE OF OUR LANDS.

It is a common saying, that plenty or scarcity of mony makes all things dear or good or cheap; and this mony is either gotton or lost in forraign trade by the over or under-ballancing of the same, as I have already shewed. It resteth now that I distinguish the seeming plenties of mony from that which is only substantial and able to perform the work: For there are divers ways and means whereby to procure plenty of mony into a Kingdom, which do not enrich but rather empoverish the same by the several inconveniences which ever accompany such alterations.

As first, if we melt down our plate into Coyn (which suits not with the Majesty of so great a Kingdom, except in cases of great extremity) it would cause Plenty of mony for a time, yet should we be nothing the richer, but rather this treasure being thus altered is made the more apt to be carried out of the Kingdom, if we exceed our means by excess in forraign wares, or maintain a war by Sea or Land, where we do not feed and cloath the Souldier and supply the armies with our own native provisions, by which disorders our treasure will soon be exhausted.

Again, if we think to bring in store of money by suffering forraign Coins to pass current at higher rates than their intrinsick value compared with our Standard, or by debasing or by enhancing our own moneys, all these have their several inconveniences and difficulties, (which hereafter I will declare) but admitting that by this means plenty of money might be brought into the Realm, yet should we be nothing the richer, neither can such treasure so gotten long remain with us. For if the stranger or the English Merchants bring in this money, it must be done upon a valuable consideration, either for wares carried out already, or after to be exported, which helps us nothing except the evil occasions of excess or war afore-named be removed which do exhaust our treasure: for otherwise, what one man bringeth for gain, another man shall be forced to carry out for necessity; because there shall ever be a necessity to ballance our Accounts with strangers, although it should be done with loss upon the rate of the money, and Confiscation also if it be intercepted by the Law.

The conclusion of this business is

briefly thus. That as the treasure which is brought into the Realm by the ballance of our forraign trade is that money which onely doth abide with us, and by which we are enriched: so by this plenty of money thus gotten (and no otherwise) do our Lands improve. For when the Merchant hath a good dispatch beyond the Seas for his Cloth and other wares, he doth presently return to buy up the greater quantity, which raiseth the price of our Woolls and other commodities, and consequently doth improve the Landlords Rents as the Leases expire daily: And also by this means money being gained, and brought more abundantly into the Kingdom, it doth enable many men to buy Lands, which will make them the dearer. But if our forraign trade come to a stop or declination by neglect at home or injuries abroad, whereby the Merchants are impoverished, and thereby the wares of the Realm less issued, then do all the said benefits cease, and our Lands fall of price daily.

How we must get Treasure to make it our own.

VI

THE SPANISH TREASURE CANNOT BE KEPT FROM OTHER KINGDOMS BY ANY PROHIBITION MADE IN SPAIN.

VI

THE SPANISH TREASURE CANNOT BE KEPT FROM OTHER KINGDOMS BY ANY PROHIBITION MADE IN SPAIN.

All the Mines of Gold and Silver which are as yet discovered in the sundry places of the world, are not of so great value as those of the West-Indies which are in the possession of the King of Spain: who thereby is enabled not onely to keep in subjection many goodly States and Provinces in Italy and elsewhere, (which otherwise would soon fall from his obeisance) but also by a continual war taking his advantage doth still enlarge his Dominions, ambitiously aiming at a Monarchy by the power of his Moneys, which are the very sinews of his strength, that lies so far dispersed into so many Countreys, yet hereby united and his wants supplied both for war and peace in a plentiful manner from all the parts of Christendom, which are therefore partakers of his treasure by a Necessity of

The policie and benefit of Spain by the trade to the East-Indies.

Commerce; wherein the Spanish policy hath ever endeavoured to prevent all other Nations the most it could: for finding Spain to be too poor and barren to supply it self and the West Indies with those varieties of forraign wares whereof they Stand in need, they knew well that when their Native Commodities come short to this purpose, their Moneys must serve to make up the reckoning; whereupon they found an incredible advantage to adde the traffick of the East-Indies to the treasure of the West: for the last of these being employed in the first, they stored themselves infinitely with rich wares to barter with all the parts of Christendom for their Commodities, and so furnishing their own necessities, prevented others for carrying away their moneys: which in point of state they hold less dangerous to impart to the remote Indians, than to their neighbour Princes, lest it should too much enable them to resist (if not offend) their enemies. And this Spanish policy against others is the more remarkable, being done likewise so much to their own advantage; for every Ryal of Eight which they sent to the East-Indies brought home so much wares as saved them the disbursing of five Ryals of Eight here in Europe (at the least) to their Neighbours, especially at those times when that trade was only in their hands: but now this great profit is failed, and the mischief removed by the English, Dutch, and others which partake in those East-India trades as ample as the Spanish Subjects.

It is further to be considered, that beside the disability of the Spaniards by their native commodities to provide forraign wares for their necessities, (whereby they are obliged to supply the want with mony) they have likewise that canker of war, which doth infinitely exhaust their treasure, and disperse it into Christendom even to their enemies, part by reprisal, but especially through a necessary maintenance of those armies which are composed of strangers, and lie so fair remote, that they cannot feed, clothe, or otherwise provide them out of their own native means and provisions, but must receive this relief from other Nations: which kind of war is far different to that which a Prince maketh upon his own confines, or in his Navies by Sea, where the Souldier receiving money for his wages, must every day deliver it out again for his necessities, whereby the treasure remains still in the Kingdom, although it be exhausted from the King: But we see that the Spaniard (trusting in the power of his Treasure) undertakes wars in Germany, and in other remote places, which would soon begger the richest Kingdom in Christendom of all their mony; the want whereof would presently disorder and bring their armies to confusion, as it falleth out sometimes with Spain it self, who have the Fountain of mony, when either it is stopt in the passage by the force of their enemies, or drawn out faster than it flows by

The effects of different wars concerning Treasure.

their own occasions; whereby also we often see that Gold and silver is so scant in Spain, that they are forced to use base copper money, to the great confusion of their Trade, and not without the undoing also of many of their own people.

But now that we have seen the occasions by which the Spanish treasure is dispersed into so many places of the world, let us likewise discover how and in what proportion each Countrey doth enjoy these Moneys, for we find that Turkey and divers other Nations have great plenty thereof, although they drive no trade with Spain, which seems to contradict the former reason, where we say that this treasure is obtained by a Necessity of Commerce. But to clear this point, we must know that all Nations (who have no Mines of their own) are enriched with Gold and Silver by one and the same means, which is already shewed to be the ballance of their forraign Trade: And this is not strictly tyed to be done in those Countries where the fountain of treasure is, but rather with such order and observations as are prescribed. For suppose England by trade with Spain may gain and bring home five hundred thousand Ryals of 8. yearly, if we lose as much by our trade in Turkey, and therefore carry the mony thither, it is not then the English, but the Turks which have got this treasure, although they have no trade with Spain from whence it was first brought. Again, if England having thus lost with Turkey do notwithstanding gain twice as much by France, Italy, and other members of her general trade, then will there remain five hundred thousand Ryals of eight cleer gains by the ballance of this trade: and this comparison holds between all other Nations, both for the manner of getting, and the proportion that is yearly gotten.

But if yet a question should be made, whether all Nations get treasure and Spain only lose it? I answer no; for some Countreys by war or by excess do lose that which they had gotten, as well as Spain by war and want of wares doth lose that which was its own.

VII

THE DIVERSITY OF GAIN BY FORRAIGN TRADE.

VII

THE DIVERSITY OF GAIN BY FORRAIGN TRADE.

In the course of forraign trade there are three sorts of gain, the first is that of the Commonwealth, which may be done when the Merchant (who is the principal Agent therein) shall lose. The second is the gain of the Merchant, which he doth sometimes justly and worthily effect, although the Commonwealth be a loser. The third is the gain of the King, whereof he is ever certain, even when the Commonwealth and the Merchant shall be both losers.

Concerning the first of these, we have already sufficiently shewed the ways and means whereby a Commonwealth may be enriched in the course of trade, whereof it is needless here to make any repetition, only I do in this place affirm, that such happiness may be in the Commonwealth, when the Merchant in his particular shall have no occasion to rejoyce. As for example, suppose the East-India Company send out one hundred thousand pounds into the East-Indies, and receive home for the same the full value of three hundred thousand pounds; Hereby it is evident that this part of the Commonwealth is trebled, and yet I may boldly say that which I can well prove, that the said Company of Merchants shall lose at least fifty thousand pounds by such an adventure if the returns be made in Spice, Indico, Callicoes, Benjamin, refined Saltpeter, and such other bulkey wares in their several proportions according to their vent and use in these parts of Europe. For the fraight of Shipping, the ensurance of the adventure, the charges of Factors abroad and Officers at home, the forbearance of the Stock, His Majesties Customs and Imposts, with other petty charges incident, cannot be less than two hundred and fifty thousand pounds, which being added to the principal produceth the said loss. And thus we see, that not only the Kingdom but also the King by his Customs and Imposts may get notoriously, even when the Merchant notwithstanding shall lose grievously; which giveth us good occasion here to consider, how much more the Realm is enriched by this noble Trade, when all things pass so happily that the Merchant is a gainer also with the King and Kingdom.

In the next place I affirm, that a Merchant by his laudable endeavours may both carry out and bring in wares to his advantage by selling them and buying them to good profit, which is the end of his labours; when nevertheless the Commonwealth shall decline and grow poor by a disorder in the people, when through Pride and other Excesses they do consume more forraign wares in value than the wealth of the Kingdom can satisfie and pay by the exportation of our own commodities, which is the very quality of an unthrift who spends beyond his means.

Lastly, the King is ever sure to get by trade, when both the Commonwealth and Merchant shall lose severally as afore-written, or joyntly, as it may and doth sometimes happen, when at one and the same time our Commodities are over-ballanced by forraign wares consumed, and that the Merchants success prove no better than is before declared.

But here we must not take the Kings gain in this large sense, for so we might say that His Majesty should get, although half the trade of the Kingdom were lost; we will rather suppose that whereas the whole trade of the Realm for Exportations and Importations is now found for to be about the yearly value of four millions and a half of pounds; it may be yet increased two hundred thousand pounds per annum more by the importation and consumption of forraign wares. By this means we know that the King shall be a gainer near twenty thousand pounds, but the Commonwealth shall lose the whole two hundred thousand pounds thus spent in excess. And the Merchant may be a loser also when the trade shall in this manner be increased to the profit of the King; who notwithstanding shall be sure in the end to have the greatest loss, if he prevent not such unthrifty courses as do impoverish his Subjects.

VIII

THE ENHANCING OR DEBASING OUR MONEYS CANNOT ENRICH THE KINGDOM WITH TREASURE, NOR HINDER THE EXPORTATION THEREOF.

VIII

THE ENHANCING OR DEBASING OUR MONEYS CANNOT ENRICH THE KINGDOM WITH TREASURE, NOR HINDER THE EXPORTATION THEREOF.

There are three ways by which the Moneys of a Kingdom are commonly altered. The first is when the Coins in their several Denominations are made current at more or less pounds, shillings or pence than formerly. The second is when the said Coins are altered in their weight, and yet continue currant at the former rates. The third is when the Standard is either debased or enriched in the fineness of the Gold and Silver, yet the Moneys continue in their former values.

In all occasions of want or plenty of Money in the Kingdom we do ever find divers men, who using their wits for a remedy to supply the first and preserve the last, they fall presently upon altering the moneys; for, say they, the raising of the Coins in value will cause it to be brought into the Realm from divers places in hope of the gain: and the debasing of the monies in the fineness or weight will keep it here for fear of the loss. But these men pleasing themselves with the beginning onely of this weighty business, consider not the progress and end thereof, whereunto we ought especially to direct our thoughts and endeavours.

Mony is the measure of our other means.

For we must know, that mony is not only the true measure of all our other means in the Kingdom, but also of our forraign commerce with strangers, which therefore ought to be kept just and constant to avoid those confusions which ever accompany such alterations. For first at home, if the common measure be changed, our Lands, Leases, wares, both forraign and domestique must alter in proportion: and although this is not done without much trouble and damage also to some men, yet in short time this must necessarily come to pass; for that is not the denomination of our pounds shillings and pence, which is respected, but the intrinsique value of our Coins; unto which we have little reason to add any further estimation or worth, if it lay in our power to do it, for this would be a special service to Spain, and an act against our selves to indear the commodity of another Prince. Neither can these courses which so much hurt the Subjects, any way help the King as some men have imagined: for although the debasing or lightning of all our

A notable service for Spain.

mony should bring a present benefit (for once only) to the Mint, yet all this and more would soon be lost again in the future great In-comes of His Majesty, when by this means they must be paid yearly with mony of less intrinsique value then formerly; Nor can it be said that the whole loss of the Kingdom would be the profit of the King, they differ infinitely: for all mens estates (be it leases, lands, debts, wares or mony) must suffer in their proportions, whereas His Majesty should have the gain only upon so much ready mony as might be new Coined, which in comparison, would prove a very small matter: for although they who have other estates in mony are said to be a great number, and to be worth five or ten thousand l. per man, more or less, which amounts to many millions in all, yet are they not possessed thereof all together or at once, for it were vanity and against their profit to keep continually in their hands above forty or fifty pounds in a family to defray necessary charges, the rest must ever run from man to man in traffique for their benefit, whereby we may conceive that a little mony (being made the measure of all our other means) doth rule and distribute great matters daily to all men in their just proportions: And we must know likewise that much of our old mony is worn light, and therefore would yield little or no profit at the Mint, and the gain upon the heavy, would cause our vigilant neighbours to carry over a great part thereof, and return it

All the ready mony in the Kingdom is esteemed at little more than one million of pounds.

presently in pieces of the new stamp: nor do we doubt that some of our own Countrymen would turn Coiners and venter a hanging for this profit, so that His Majesty in the end should get little by such alterations.

Yea but say some men, If His Majesty raise the mony, great store of treasure would also be brought into the Mint from forraign parts, for we have seen by experience that the late raising of our Gold ten in the hundred, did bring in great store thereof, more than we were accustomed to have in the Kingdom, the which as I cannot deny, so do I likewise affirm, that this Gold carried away all or the most part of our Silver, (which was not over-worn or too light) as we may easily perceive by the present use of our Moneys in their respective qualities; and the reason of this change is, because our Silver was not raised in proportion with our Gold, which still giveth advantage to the Merchant to bring in the Kingdoms yearly gain by trade in Gold rather than in Silver.

Secondly, if we be inconstant in our Coins, and thereby violate the Laws of forraign Commerce; other Princes are vigilant in these cases to alter presently in proportion with us, and then where is our hope? or if they do not alter, what can we hope for? For if the stranger-merchant bring in his wares, and find that our moneys are raised, shall not he likewise keep his Commodities untill he may sell them dearer? and shall not the price of the

Merchants exchange with forraign Countries rise in proportion with our Moneys? All which being undoubtedly true, why may not our Moneys be carried out of the Kingdom as well and to as much profit after the raising thereof, as before the alteration?

But peradventure some men will yet say, that if our Moneys be raised and other Countries raise not, it will cause more Bullion and forraign Coines to be brought in than heretofore. If this be done, it must be performed either by the Merchant who hath exported wares, or by the Merchant who intends to buy off our Commodities: and it is manifest that neither of these can have more advantage or benefit by this Art now, than they might have had before the alteration of the Money. For if their said Bullion and forraign Coins be more worth than formerly in our pounds, shillings and pence, yet what shall they get by that when these moneys are baser or lighter, and that therefore they are risen in proportion? So we may plainly see that these Innovations are no good means to bring treasure into the Kingdom, nor yet to keep it here when we have it.

IX

A TOLERATION FOR FORRAIGN COINS TO PASS CURRANT HERE AT HIGHER RATES THAN THEIR VALUE WITH OUR STANDARD, WILL NOT ENCREASE OUR TREASURE.

IX

A TOLERATION FOR FORRAIGN COINS TO PASS CURRANT HERE AT HIGHER RATES THAN THEIR VALUE WITH OUR STANDARD, WILL NOT ENCREASE OUR TREASURE.

Merchants do or ought to know the weight and fineness of forraign Coins.

THE discreet Merchant for the better directing of his trade and his exchanges by bills to and from the several places of the world where he is acustomed to deal, doth carefully learn the Parity or equal value of the monies according to their weight and fineness compared with our Standard, whereby he is able to know perfectly the just profit or loss of his affairs. And I make no doubt but that we trade to divers places where we vent off our native commodities yearly, to a great value, and yet find few or no wares there fitting our use, whereby we are enforced to make our returns in ready mony, which by us is either carried into some other Countries to be converted into wares which we want, or else it is brought into the Realm in Specie;

which being tolerated to pass current here in payment at higher rates than they are worth to be Coined into sterling mony; that seemeth very probable that the greater quantity will be brought in: but when all the circumstances are duly considered, this course likewise will be found as weak as the rest to encrease our Treasure.

First, the toleration it self doth break the laws of entercourse, and would soon move other Princes to perform the same acts or worse against us, and so frustrate our hopes.

Secondly, if mony be the true measure of all our other means, and forraign Coins tollerated to pass current amongst us, at higher rates than they are worth (being compared with our Standard) it followeth that the common wealth shall not be justly distributed, when it passeth by a false measure.

Thirdly, if the advantage between ours and forraign Coins be but small, it will bring in little or no Treasure, because the Merchant will rather bring in wares upon which there is usually a competent gaine. And on the other side if we permit a great advantage to the forraign Coins, then that gain will carry away all our starling mony, and so I leave this business in a Dilemma, and fruitless, as all other courses will ever prove which seek for the gain or loss of our treasure out of the ballance of our general forraign trade, as I will endeavour yet further to demonstrate.

X

THE OBSERVATION OF THE STATUTE OF IMPLOYMENTS TO BE MADE BY STRANGERS, CANNOT ENCREASE, NOR YET PRESERVE OUR TREASURE.

X

THE OBSERVATION OF THE STATUTE OF IMPLOYMENTS TO BE MADE BY STRANGERS, CANNOT ENCREASE, NOR YET PRESERVE OUR TREASURE.

To keep our mony in the Kingdom is a work of no less skill and difficulty than to augment our Treasure: for the causes of their preservation and production are the same in nature. The statute for employment of strangers wares into our commodities seemeth at the first to be a good and a lawful way leading to those ends; but upon th' examination of the particulars; we shall find that it cannot produce such good effects.

The use of Forraign Trade is alike to all Nations.

For as the use of forraign trade is alike unto all Nations, so may we easily perceive what will be done therein by strangers, when we do but observe our own proceedings in this waighty business, by which we do not only seek with the vent of our own commodities to supply our wants of forraign wares, but also to enrich our selves with treasure: all which is done by a different manner of trading according to our own occasions and the nature of the places whereunto we do trade; as namely in some Countrys we sell our commodities and bring away their wares, or part in mony; in other Countreys we sell our goods and take their mony, because they have little or no wares that fits our turns: again in some places we have need of their commodities, but they have little use of ours: so they take our mony which we get in other Countreys: And thus by a course of traffick (which changeth according to the accurrents of time) the particular members do accommodate each other, and all accomplish the whole body of the trade, which will ever languish if the harmony of her health be distempered by the diseases of excess at home, violence abroad, charges and restrictions at home or abroad: but in this place I have occasion to speak only of restriction, which I will perform briefly.

How forraign trade is destroyed.

There are three ways by which a Merchant may make the returns of his wares from beyond the Seas, that is to say in mony, in commodities, or by Exchange. But the Statute of employment doth not only restrain mony (in which there is a seeming providence and Justice) but also the use of the Exchange by bills, which doth violate the Law of Commerce, and is indeed an Act without example in any place of the world where we have trade, and therefore to be considered, that whatsoever (in this kind) we shall impose upon strangers here, will presently be made a Law for us in their Countreys, especially where we have our greatest trade with our vigilant neighbours, who omit no care nor occasion to support their traffique in equal privileges with other Nations. And thus in the first place we should be deprived of that freedom and means which now we have to bring Treasure into the Kingdom, and therewith likewise we should lose the vent of much wares which we carry to divers places, whereby our trade and our Treasure would decay together.

Secondly, if by the said Statute we thrust the exportation of our wares (more than ordinary) upon the stranger, we must then take it from the English, which were injurious to our Merchants, Marriners and Shipping, besides the hurt to the Commonwealth in venting the Kingdoms stock to the stranger at far lower rates here than we must do if we sold it to them in their own Countrys, as is proved in the third Chapter.

Thirdly, whereas we have already sufficiently shewed, that if our commodities be over ballanced in value by forraign wares, our mony must be carried out. How is it possible to prevent this by tying the Strangers hands, and leaving the English loose? shall not the same reasons and advantage cause that to be done by them now, that was done by the other before? or if we will make a statute (without example) to prevent both alike, shall we not then overthrow all at once? the King in his customes and the Kingdom in her profits; for such a restriction must of necessity destroy much trade, because the diversity of occasions and places which make an ample trade require that some men should both export and import wares; some export only, others import, some deliver out their monies by exchange, others take it up; some carry out mony, others bring it in, and this is a greater or lesser quantity according to the good husbandry or excess in the Kingdom, over which only if we keep a strict law, it will rule all the rest, and without this all other Statutes are no rules either to keep or procure us Treasure.

Lastly, to leave no Objection unanswered, if it should be said that a Statute comprehending the English as well as the stranger must needs keep our money in the Kingdom. What shall we get by this, if it hinder the coming in of money by the decay of that ample Trade which we enjoyed in the freedom thereof? is not the Remedy far worse than the Disease? shall we not live more like Irishmen than Englishmen, when the Kings revenues, our Merchants, Mariners, Shipping, Arts, Lands, Riches, and all decay together with our Trade?

Yea but, say some men, we have better hopes than so; for th' intent of the Statute is, that as all the forraign wares which are brought in shall be imployed in our commodities, thereby to keep our money in the Kingdom:

So we doubt not but to send out a sufficient quantity of our own wares over and above to bring in the value thereof in ready money.

Although this is absolutely denied by the reasons afore written, yet now we will grant it, because we desire to end the dispute: For if this be true, that other Nations will vent more of our commodities than we consume of theirs in value, then I affirm that the overplus must necessarily return unto us in treasure without the use of the Statute, which is therefore not onely fruitless but hurtful, as some other like restrictions are found to be when they are fully discovered.

XI

IT WILL NOT INCREASE OUR TREASURE TO ENJOYN THE MERCHANT THAT EXPORTETH FISH, CORN OR MUNITION, TO RETURN ALL OR PART OF THE VALUE IN MONEY.

XI

IT WILL NOT INCREASE OUR TREASURE TO ENJOYN THE MERCHANT THAT EXPORTETH FISH, CORN OR MUNITION, TO RETURN ALL OR PART OF THE VALUE IN MONEY.

Victuals and Munitions for war are so pretious in a Commonwealth, that either it seemeth necessary to restrain the exportation altogether, or (if the plenty permits it) to require the return thereof in so much treasure; which appeareth to be reasonable and without difficulty, because Spain and other Countries do willingly part with their money for such wares, although in other occasions of trade they straightly prohibit the exportation thereof: all which I grant to be true, yet notwithstanding we must consider that all the ways and means which (in course of trade) force treasure into the Kingdom, do not therefore make it ours: for this can be done onely by a lawful gain, and this gain is no way to be accomplished but by the overballance of our trade, and this overballance is made less by restrictions: therefore such restrictions do hinder the increase of our treasure. The Argument is plain, and needs no other reasons to strengthen it, except any man be so vain to think that restrictions would not cause the less wares to be exported. But if this likewise should be granted, yet to enjoyn the Merchant to bring in money for Victuals and Munition carried out, will not cause us to have one peny the more in the Kingdom at the years end; for whatsoever is forced in one way must out again another way: because onely so much will remain and abide with us as is gained and incorporated into the estate of the Kingdom by the overbalance of the trade.

Some restrictions hinder Trade.

This may be made plain by an example taken from an Englishman, who had occasion to buy and consume the wares of divers strangers for the value of six hundred pounds, and having wares of his own for the value of one thousand pounds, he sold them to the said strangers, and presently forced all the mony from them into his own power; yet upon cleering of the reckoning between them there remained onely four hundred pounds to the said Englishman for overballance of the wares bought and sold; so the rest which he had received from returned back from whence he forced it. And this shall suffice to shew that whatsoever courses we take to force money into the Kingdom, yet so much onely will remain with us as we shall gain by the ballance of our trade.

XII

THE UNDERVALUING OF OUR MONEY WHICH IS DELIVERED OR RECEIVED BY BILLS OF EXCHANGE HERE OR BEYOND THE SEAS, CANNOT DECREASE OUR TREASURE.

XII

THE UNDERVALUING OF OUR MONEY WHICH IS DELIVERED OR RECEIVED BY BILLS OF EXCHANGE HERE OR BEYOND THE SEAS, CANNOT DECREASE OUR TREASURE.

The Merchants Exchange by Bills is a means and practice whereby they that have money in one Countrey may deliver the same to receive it again in another Countrey at certain times and rates agreed upon, whereby the lender and the borrower are accommodated without transporting of treasure from State to State.

These Exchanges thus made between man and man, are not contracted at the equal value of the moneys, according to their respective weights and fineness: First, because he that delivereth his money doth respect the venture of the debt, and the time of forbearance; but that which causeth an under or overvaluing of moneys by Exchange, is the plenty or scarcity thereof in those places where the Exchanges are made. For example, when here is plenty of money to be delivered for Amsterdam, then shall our money be undervalued in Exchange, because they who take up the money, seeing it so plentifully thrust upon them, do thereby make advantage to themselves in taking the same at an undervalue.

And contrariwise, when here is scarcity of mony to be delivered for Amsterdam, the deliverer will make the same advantage by overvaluing our money which he delivereth. And thus we see that as plenty or scarcity of mony in a Commonwealth doth make all things dear or good cheap: so in the course of exchange it hath ever a contrary working; wherefore in the next place it is fit to set down the true causes of this effect.

Plenty of Mony makes the Exchange cheap, and all other things dear.

As plenty or scarcity of mony do make the price of the exchange high or low, so the over or under ballance of our trade doth effectually cause the plenty or scarcity of mony: And here we must understand, that the ballance of our trade is either General or Particular. The General is, when all our yearly traffique is jointly valued, as I have formerly shewed; the particular is when our trade to Italy, France, Turkey, Spain, and other Countreys are severally considered: and by this latter course we shall perfectly find out the places where our mony is under or overvalued in Exchange: For although our general exportations of wares may be yearly more in value than that which is imported, whereby the difference is made good to us in so much treasure: nevertheless the particular trades do work diversly: For peradventure the Low Countreys may bring us more in value than we sell them, which if it be so, then do the Low Countrey Merchants not only carry away our treasure to ballance the accompt between us, but also by this means mony being plentiful here to be delivered by exchange, it is therefore undervalued by the takers, as I have before declared; And contrariwise if we carry more wares to Spain, and other places than we consume of theirs, then do we bring away their treasure, and likewise in the Merchants exchange we overvalue our own money.

What kinds of plenty or scarcity of mony make the Exchange high or low.

Yet still there are some who will seem to make this plain by Demonstration, that the undervaluing of our money by Exchange doth carry it out of the Kingdom: for, say they, we see daily great store of our English Coins carried over, which pass current in the Low-Countries, and there is great advantage to carry them thither, to save the loss which the Low-Countrymen have in the Exchange; for if one hundred pounds sterling delivered here, is so much undervalued, that ninty pounds of the same sterling money carried over in specie shall be sufficient to make repaiment and full satisfaction of the said hundred pounds at Amsterdam: It is not then (say they) the undervaluing of our Mony which causeth it to be carried out of the Realm?

To this Objection I will make a full and plain Answer, shewing that it is not the undervaluing of our money in exchange, but the overballancing of our trade that canieth away our treasure. For suppose that our whole trade with the Low-Countries for wares brought into this Realm be performed onely by the Dutch for the value of five hundred thousand pounds yearly; and that all our commodities transported into the said Low-Countries be performed onely by the English for four hundred thousand pounds yearly: Is it not then manifest, that the Dutch can exchange only four hundred thousand pounds with the English upon the Par pro pari or equal value of the respective Standards? So the other hundred thousand pounds which is the overballance of the trade, they must of necessity carry away that in mony. And the self same loss of treasure must happen if there were no exchange at all permitted: for the Dutch carrying away our mony for their wares, and we bringing in their forraign Coins for their commodities, there will be still one hundred thousand pounds loss.

Now let us add another example grounded upon the aforesaid proportion of trade between us and the Low Countreys. The Dutch (as afore-written) may exchange with the English for four hundred thousand pounds and no more upon the equal value of the monies, because the English have no further means to satisfie. But now suppose that in respect of the plenty of mony, which in this case will be here in the hands of the Dutch to deliver by exchange, our mony (according to that which hath been already said) be strangers Undervalued ten per cent. then is it manifest that the Dutch must deliver four hundred and forty thousand pounds to have the Englishmans four hundred thousand pounds in the Low Countreys: so that there will then remain but 60000. pounds for the Dutch to carry out of the Realm to ballance the accompt between them and us. Whereby we may plainly perceive that the undervaluing of our money in exchange, will not carry it out of the Kingdom, as some men have supposed, but rather is a means to make a less quantity thereof to be exported, than would be done at the Par pro pari.

The undervaluing of our mony in Exchange is the Strangers loss and our gain.

Further let us suppose that the English Merchant carrieth out as much wares in value as the Dutch Merchant bringeth in, whereby the means is equal between them to make their returns by exchange without carrying away of any mony to the prejudice of either State. And yet notwithstanding the Dutch Merchant for his occasions or advantage will forsake this course of exchange, and will venture to send part of his returns in ready mony.

To this the answer is, that hereupon it must follow of necessity, that the Dutch shall want just so much means in exchange with the English, who therefore shall be forced to bring in the like sum of mony from beyond the Seas, as the Dutch carried out of this Realm; so that we may plainly perceive that the monies which are carried from us within the ballance of our trade are not considerable, for they do return to us again: and we lose those monies only which are made of the overballance of our general trade, that is to say, That which we spend more in value in forraign wares, than we utter of our own commodities. And the contrary of this is the only means by which we get our treasure. In vain therefore hath Gerard Malines laboured so long, and in so many printed books to make the world beleeve that the undervaluing of our money in exchange doth exhaust our treasure, which is a mere fallacy of the cause, attributing that to a Secondary means, whose effects are wrought by another Principal Efficient, and would also come to pass although the said Secondary means were not at all. As vainly also hath he propounded a remedy by keeping the price of Exchange by Bills at the par pro pari by publick Authority, which were a newfound Office without example in any part of the world, being not only fruitless but also hurtful, as hath been sufficiently proved in this Chapter, and therefore I will proceed to the next.

1. The Canker of Englands Commonwealth. 2. Free trade. 3. Lex Mercatoria. 4. The Centre of trade.

XIII

THE MERCHANT WHO IS A MERE EXCHANGER OF MONEY BY BILLS CANNOT INCREASE OR DECREASE OUR TREASURE.

XIII

THE MERCHANT WHO IS A MERE EXCHANGER OF MONEY BY BILLS CANNOT INCREASE OR DECREASE OUR TREASURE.

There are certain Merchants which deal onely upon all advantages in th' Exchange, and neither export nor import wares into the Kingdom, which hath caused some men to affirm, that the money which such mere Exchangers bring in or carry out of the Realm is not comprehended in the ballance of our forraign trade; for (say they) sometimes when our sterling mony hath been undervalued and delivered here for Amsterdam at ten. per cent. less than the equal value of the respective Standards, the said mere Exchanger may take here one thousand pounds sterling & carry over onely nine hundred thereof in specie, which will be sufficient to pay his Bill of Exchange. And so upon a greater or a lesser summe the like gain is made in three months time.

But here we must know, that although this mere Exchanger deal not in wares, yet notwithstanding the money which he carrieth away in manner afore-written must necessarily proceed of such wares as are brought into the Kingdom by Merchants. So that still it falleth into the ballance of our forraign trade, and worketh the same effect, as if the Merchant himself had carried away that money, which he must do if our wares be overballanced, as ever they are when our money is undervalued, which is expressed more at large in the 12. Chapter.

And on the contrary, when the mere Exchanger (by the said advantages) shall bring money into the Kingdom, he doth no more than necessarily must be done by the Merchant himself when our commodities overbalance forraign wares. But in these occasions some Merchants had rather lose by delivering their money at an under-value in Exchange, than undertake to hazard all by the Law; which notwithstanding these mere Exchangers will perform for them in hope of gain.

XIV

THE ADMIRABLE FEATS SUPPOSED TO BE DONE BY BANKERS AND THE MERCHANTS EXCHANGE.

XIV

THE ADMIRABLE FEATS SUPPOSED TO BE DONE BY BANKERS AND THE MERCHANTS EXCHANGE.

Although I have already written something concerning the Merchants Exchange, and therein of the undervaluation of our money, and of the mere Exchanger, with their true causes and effects; Nevertheless it will not be impertinent to pursue this business a little further, and thereby not onely to strengthen our former Arguments, but also to avoid some cunning delusions which might deceive the unskilful Reader of those books entituled, Lex Mercatoria, pag. 409. and The maintenance of free trade, pag. 16. wherein the Author Gerard Malynes setteth down the admirable feats (as he termeth them) which are to be done by Bankers and Exchangers, with the use and power of the exchange: but how these wonders may be effected he altogether omitteth, leaving the Reader in a strange opinion of these dark mysteries, which I cannot think he did for want of knowledge, for I find him skilful in many things which he hath both written and collected concerning th' affairs of Merchants, and in particular he discourses well of divers uses, forms and passages of the Exchange, in all which as he hath taken great pains for the good of others, so do his Works of this kind deserve much praise: but where he hath disguised his own knowledge with Sophistry to further some private ends by hurting the publick good; there ought he to be discovered and prevented, unto which performance (in this discourse of treasure) I find my self obliged, and therefore I intend to effect it by shewing the true causes and means whereby these wonders are done, which Malines attributeth to the sole power of the Exchange. But first for order I think it fit to set down the particular feats as they stand in his said books.

The admirable feats to be done by Exchange.

1. To lay their mony with gain in any place of the world where any exchange lyeth.

2. To gain and wax rich, and never meddle with any Princes commodities.

3. To buy any Princes commodity, and never bring penny nor pennyworth into the Realm, but doe that with the Subjects mony.

4. To grow rich and live without adventure at Sea or travaile.

5. To do great feats having credit, and yet to be nought worth.

6. To understand whether in conjecture their mony employed on Exchange, or buying of wares will be more profit.

7. To know certainly what the Merchants gain upon their wares they sell and buy.

8. To live and encrease upon every Princes subjects that continually take up mony by Exchange, and whether they gain or no.

9. To wind out every Princes treasure out of his Realm whose Subjects bring in more wares than they carry out of the Realm.

10. To make the Staple of money run thither where the rich Princes will have it to be bought, and pay for it.

11. To unfurish the poor Prince of his provision of mony, that keeps his wares upon interest mony, if the enemy will seek it.

12. To furnish their need of mony that tarry the selling of their wares in any Contract untill they make them come to their price.

13. To take up mony to engross any commodity either new come or whereof they have some store to bring the whole trade of that commodity into their own hands to sell both at their pleasure.

14. To hide their carrying away of any Princes mony.

15. To fetch away any Princes fine mony with his own or any other Princes base mony.

16. To take up Princes base mony and to turn into his fine mony, and to pay the deliverer with his own, and gain too.

17. To take upon credit into their hands for a time all the Merchants mony that will be delivered, and pay them with their own, and gain too.

18. To make the Realm gain of all other Realms whose Subjects live most by their own commodities, and sell yearly the overplus into the world, and both occupie that encrease yearly, and also their old store of treasure upon exchange.

19. To undoe Realms and Princes that look not to their Commonwealth, when the Merchants wealth is such, that the great houses conspire together so to rule the Exchange,

that when they will be deliverers, they will receive in another place above the Standard of the Mint of the Princes mony delivered: and when they will be takers, they will pay the same in another place under the Standard of the Mint of the Princes mony taken up.

20. To get ready mony to buy any commodity that is offered cheap.

21. To compass ready mony to get any offered bargain out of another mans hands, and so by outbidding others oftentimes to raise the wares.

22. To get a part and sometimes all his gains that employeth mony taken up by Exchange in wares, and so make others travail for their gain.

23. To keep Princes for having any Customs, Subsidies or Taxes upon their mony, as they employ it not.

24. To value justly any Wares they carry into any Countrey by setting them at that value, as the mony that bought them was then at by Exchange in the Countrey whither they be carried.

If I had a desire to amplifie in the explanation of these wonders, they would afford me matter enough to make a large volume, but my intent is to do it as briefly as possibly I may without obscurity. And before I begin, I cannot chuse but laugh to think how a worthy Lawyer might be dejected in his laudable studies, when he should see more cunning in Lex Mercatoria by a little part of the Merchants profession, than in all the Law-cases of his learned Authors: for this Exchange goes beyond Conjuring; I think verily that neither Doctor Faustus nor Banks his Horse could ever do such admirable feats, although it is sure they had a Devil to help them; but wee Merchants deal not with such Spirits, we delight not to be thought the workers of lying wonders, and therefore I endeavour here to shew the plainness of our dealing (in these supposed feats) to be agreeable to the laudable course of Trade.

And first, To lay our money with gaine to any place of the World where Exchange lieth. How can this be done (will some men say) for Amsterdam, when the losse by Exchange is sometimes eight or ten per cent. more or lesse for one moneths usance? The answer is, That here I must consider, first, that the principal efficient cause of this losse, is a greater value in Wares brought from Amsterdam then we carry thither, which make more Deliverers then Takers here by Exchange, whereby the Mony is undervalued to the benefit of the taker: hereupon the Deliverer, rather then he will lose by his Money, doth consider those Countreys, unto

The principal efficient cause of loss by Exchange.

which we carry more Wares in value then we receive from them; as namely, Spain, Italy, and others; to which places he is sure (for the reasons aforesaid) that he shall ever deliver his money with profit. But now you will say, that the money is further from Amsterdam than before; How shall it be got together? yes, well enough; and the farther about will prove the nearest way home, if it come at last with good profit; the first part whereof being made (as we have supposed) in Spain, from thence I consider where to make my second gain, and finding that the Florentines send out a greater value in cloth of Gold and Silver, wrought Silks, and Rashes to Spain, than they receive in Fleece Woolls, West-India Hides, Sugar and Cochineal, I know I cannot miss of my purpose by delivering my money for Florence; where (still upon the same ground) I direct my course from thence to Venice, and there finde that my next benefit must be at Frankfort or Antwerp, untill at last I come to Amsterdam by a shorter or longer course, according to such occasions of advantage as the times and places shall afford me. And thus we see still, that the profit and loss upon the Exchange is guided and ruled by the over or under ballance of the several Trades which are Predominant and Active, making the price of Exchange high or low, which is therefore Passive, the contrary whereof is so often repeated by the said Malynes.

To the second, fourth, fourteenth,

and twenty third, I say, that all these are the proper works of the meer Exchanger, and that his actions cannot work to the good or hurt of the Commonwealth, I have already sufficiently shewed in the last Chap. and therefore here I may spare that labour.

To the third. It is true, I can deliver one thousand pounds here by exchange to receive the value in Spaine, where with this Spanish money I can buy and bring away so much Spanish wares. But all this doth not prove, but that in the end the English money or commodities must pay for the said wares: for if I deliver my thousand pounds here to an English-man, he must pay me in Spain, either by goods already sent, or to be sent thither; or if I deliver it here to a Spaniard, he takes it of me, with intent to employ it in our wares; so that every way we must pay the Stranger for what we have from him: Is there any feats in all this worthy our admiration?

To the fifth, thirteenth, twentieth, and twenty first. I must answer these Wonders by heaps, where I finde them to be all one matter in divers formes, and such froth also, that every Idiot knowes them, and can say, that he who hath credit can contract, buy, sell, and take up much money by Exchange, which he may do as well also at Interest: yet in these courses they are not alwayes gainers, for sometimes they live by the losse, as well as they who have less credit.

To the sixth and seventh. Here is more

poor stuff; for when I know the current price of my Wares, both here and beyond the Seas, I may easily conjecture whether the profit of the Exchange or the gain which I expect upon my Wares will be greater. And again, as every Merchant knows well what he gains upon the Wares he buyeth and selleth, so may any other man do the like that can tell how the said Merchant hath proceeded: But what is all this to make us admire the Exchange?

To the eighth and twelfth. As Bankers and Exchangers do furnish men with money for their occasions, so do they likewise who let out their money at interest with the same hopes and like advantage, which many times notwithstanding fails them, as well as the Borrowers often labour onely for the Lenders profit.

To the ninth and eighteenth. Here my Author hath some secret meaning, or being conscious of his own errours, doth mark these two Wonders with a ☞ in the Margin. For why should this great work of enriching or impoverishing of Kingdomes be attributed to the Exchange, which is done onely by those means that doe over or under-ballance our Forraign Trade, as I have already so often shewed, and as the very words of Malynes himself in these two places may intimate to a judicious Reader?

To the fifteenth and sixteenth. I confess that the Exchange may be used in turning base money into Gold or Silver, as when a stranger may coin and bring over a great quantity of Farthings, which in short time he may disperse or convert into good money, and then deliver the same here by exchange to receive the value in his own Countrey; or he may do this feat by carrying away the said good mony in specie without using the exchange at all, if he dare venture the penalty of the Law. The Spaniards know well who are the common Coiners of Christendome, that dare venture to bring them store of Copper money of the Spanish stamp, and carry away the value in good Ryals of Eight, wherein notwithstanding all their cunning devices, they are sometimes taken tardie.

To the 17. The Bankers are always ready to receive such sums of mony as are put into their hands by men of all degrees, who have no skill or good means themselves to manage the same upon the exchange to profit. It is likewise true that the Bankers do repay all men with their own, and yet reserve good gain to themselves, which they do as well deserve for their ordinary provision or allowance as those Factors do which buy or sell for Merchants by Commission: And is not this likewise both just and very common?

Lex Mercatoria, pag. 410. Maintenance of free trade, p. 17.

To the II. I must confess that here is a wonder indeed, that a poor Prince should keep either his wars or wares (I take both together as the Author sets them down both ways differing in his said two books) upon interest mony; for what needs the Enemy of such a poor Prince deale with the Bankers to disappoint him or defeat him of his mony in time of want, when the interest it self will do this fast enough, and so I leave this poor stuff.

To the 19. I have lived long in Italy, where the greatest Banks and Bankers of Christendom do trade, yet could I never see nor hear, that they did, or were able to rule the price of Exchange by confederacie, but still the plenty or scarcity of mony in the course of trade did always overrule them and made the Exchanges to run at high or low rates.

Exchange hinders not Princes of their customs.

To the 22. The Exchange by bills between Merchant and Merchant in the course of trade cannot hinder Princes of their Customs and Imposts: for the mony which one man delivereth, because he will not, or hath not occasion to employ it in wares, another man taketh, because he either will or hath already laid it out in Merchandize. But it is true that when the wealth of a Kingdom consisteth much in ready mony, and that there is also good means and conveniencie in such a Kingdom to trade with the same into forraign parts, either by Sea or Land, or by both these ways; if then this trade be neglected, the King shall be defeated of those profits: and if the exchange be the cause thereof, then must we learn in what manner this is done; for we may exchange either amongst our selves, or with strangers; if amongst our selves, the Commonwealth cannot be enriched thereby; for the gain of one subject is the loss of another.

And if we exchange with strangers, then our profit is the gain of the Commonwealth. Yet by none of these ways can the King receive any benefit in his customes. Let us therefore seek out the places where such exchanging is used, and set down the reasons why this practice is permitted; in search whereof we shall only find one place of note in all Christendome, which is Genoua, whereof I intend to say something as briefly as I can.

The present estate of the commonwealth of Genoua.

The State of Genoua is small, and not very fertile, having little natural wealth or materials to employ the people, nor yet victuals sufficient to feed them; but nevertheless by their industry in former times by forraign trade into AEgypt, Soria, Constantinople, and all those Levant parts for Spices, Drugs, raw Silks and many other rich wares, with which they served the most places of Europe, they grew to an incredible wealth, which gave life unto the strength of their Cities, the pomp of their buildings, and other singular beauties. But after the foundation and encrease of that famous City of Venice, the said trades turned that way. And since likewise the greatest part thereof doth come into England, Spain, and the Low Countreys by navigation directly from the East Indies, which alterations in the traffique, hath forced them of Genoua to change their course of trading with wares, into exchanging of their mony; which for gain they spread not only into divers Countreys where the trade

is performed with Merchandize, but more especially they do therewith serve the want of the Spaniard in Flanders and other places for their wars, whereby the private Merchants are much enriched, but the publique treasure by this course is not encreased, and the reasons why the Commonwealth of Genoua doth suffer this inconvenience,
are these.

First and principally, they are forced to leave those trades which they cannot keep from other Nations, who have better means by situation, wares, Shipping, Munition and the like, to perform these affairs with more advantage than they are able to doe.

Secondly, they proceed like a wise State, who still retain as much trade as they can, although they are not able to procure the twentieth part of that which they had. For having few or no materials of their own to employ their people, yet they supply this want by the Fleece-wools of Spain, and raw Silks of Sicilia, working them into Velvets, Damasks, Sattens, Woollen-drapery, and other manufactures.

Thirdly, whereas they find no means in their own Countrey to employ and trade their great wealth to profit, they content themselves to do it in Spain and other places, either for Merchandize, or by exchanging their monies for gain to those Merchants who trade therewith in wares. And thus wheresoever they live abroad for a time circuiting the world for gain; yet in the end the Center of this profit is in their own Native Countrey.

Lastly, the government of Genoua being Aristocracie, they are assured that although the publique get little, yet if their private Merchants gain much from strangers, they shall doe well enough, because the richest and securest Treasure of a Free State, are the riches of the Nobility (who in Genoua are Merchants) which falleth not out so in a Monarchy, where between the comings in of a Prince, and the means of Private Men, there is this distinction of meum & tuum, but in the occasions and dangers of a Republick or Commonwealth, where Liberty and Government might be changed into Servitude, there the Proper substance of private men is the publique Treasure, ready to be spent with their lives in defence of their own Soveraignty.

To the 24. If a Merchant should buy wares here with intentions to send them for Venice, and then value them as the Exchange comes from thence to London, he may find himself far wide of his reckoning: for before his goods arrive at Venice, both the price of his Wares and the rate of the Exchange may alter very much. But if the meaning of the Author be, that this valuation may be made after the goods arrive, and are sold at Venice, and the money remitted hither by Exchange, or else the money which bought the said wares here may be valued as the Exchange passed at that time from hence to Venice; Is not all this very common and easie business, unworthy to be put into the number of Admirable feats?

To the tenth. Although a rich Prince hath great power, yet is there not power in every rich Prince to make the staple of Money run where he pleaseth: for the Staple of any thing is not where it may be had, but where the thing doth most of all abound. Whereupon we commonly say, that the Spaniard, in regard of his great treasure in the West Indies, hath the Fountain or Staple of money, which he moveth and causeth to run into Italy, Germany, the Low Countreys, or other places where his occasions doe require it, either for Peace or War. Neither is this effected by any singular Power of the Exchange, but by divers wayes and means fitting those places where the money is to be employed. For if the use thereof be upon the confines of France to maintain a War there, then may it be safely sent in specie on Carriages by Land; if in Italy, on Gallies by Sea; if in the Low Countreys, on Shipping by Sea also, but yet with more danger, in regard of his potent enemies in that passage. Wherefore in this occasion, although the Exchange is not absolutely necessary, yet it is very useful. And because the Spaniards want of Commodities from Germany and the Low Countreys is greater in value than the Spanish Wares which are carried into those parts, therefore the King of Spain cannot be furnished there from his own subjects with money by exchange, but is and hath been a long time enforc'd to carry a great part of his treasure in Gallies for Italy, where the Italians, and amongst them the Merchants of Genoua especially, do take the same, and repay the value thereof in Flanders, whereunto they are enabled by their great trade with many rich commodities which they send continually out of Italy into those Countreys and the places thereabouts, from whence the Italians return no great value in wares, but deliver their money for the service of Spain, and receive the value by Exchange in Italy out of the Spanish Treasure, which is brought thither in Gallies, as is afore-written.

How the Italians are enabled to furnish Spain with money in Flanders.

So that by this we plainly see, that it is not the power of Exchange that doth enforce treasure where the rich Prince will have it, but it is the money proceeding of wares in Forraigne trade that doth enforce the exchange, and rules the price thereof high or low, according to the plenty or scarcity of the said money; which in this discourse, upon all occasions, I think I have repeated neer as often as Malynes in his Books doth make the Exchange to be an essential part of trade, to be active, predominant, over-ruling the price of Wares and Moneys, life, spirit, and the worker of admirable feats. All which we have now briefly expounded; and let no man admire why he himself did not take this pains, for then he should not onely have taken away the great opinion which he laboured to maintain of the Exchange, but also by a true discovery of the right operation thereof, he should utterly have overthrown his par pro pari; which project (if it had prevailed) would have been a good business for the Dutch, and to the great hurt of this Common-wealth, as hath been sufficiently proved in the 12. chapter.

Now therefore let the learned Lawyer fall cheerfully to his books again, for the Merchant cannot put him down, if he have no more skill than is in his Exchange. Are these such admirable feats, when they may be so easily known and done in the course of trade? Well then, if by this discovery we have eased the Lawyers minde, and taken off the edge of his admiration, let him now play his part, and take out a Writ of Errour against the Par pro Pari; for this project hath misinformed many, and put us to trouble to expound these Riddles.

Nay, but stay awhile, can all this pass for current, to slight a business thus, which (the Author saith) hath been so seriously observed by that famous Council, and those worthy Merchants of Elizabeth of blessed memory, and also condemned by those French Kings, Lewis the 9th, Philip the fair, and Philip de Valois, with confiscation of the Bankers goods? I must confess that all this requires an answer, which in part is already done by the Author himself. For he saith, that the wisdome of our State found out the evil, but they missed of the remedy; and yet what remedy this should be no man can tell; for there was none applyed, but all practise and use in Exchange stand still to this day in such manner and form as they did at the time when these Feats were discovered, for the State knew well that there needed no remedy where there was no disease.

Well then, how shall we be able to answer the proceedings of the French Kings who did absolutely condemn the Bankers, and confiscated their goods? Yes, well enough, for the Bankers might perhaps be condemned for something done in their exchanges against the Law, and yet their profession may still be lawful, as it is in Italy and France it self to this day. Nay we will grant likewise that the Banks were banished, when the Bankers were punished; yet all this proves nothing against Exchangers, for Kings and States enact many Statutes, and suddenly repeale them, they do and undo; Princes may err, or else Malynes is grosly mistaken, where he setteth down 35. several Statutes and other ordinances enacted by this State in 350. years time to remedy the decay of Trade, and yet all are found defective; only his reformation of the Exchange, or Par pro Pari, is effectual, if we would believe him, but we know better, and so we leave him.

Maintenance of free trade, p.76, 77, 78, nd 79.

I might here take occasion to say something against another project of the same brood that lately attended upon the success of this Par pro pari, as I have been credibly informed, which is, the changing and re-changing here within the Realm, of all the Plate, Bullion and Monies, Forraign or Sterling, to pass only by an office called, The Kings Royal Exchanger, or his Deputies, paying them a Peny upon the value of every Noble: which might raise much to their private good, and destroy more to the publique hurt. For it would decay the Kings Coinage, deprive the Kingdom of much Treasure, abridge the Subjects of their just liberty, and utterly overthrow the worthy trade of the Goldsmiths, all which being plain and easie to the weakest understandings, I will therefore omit to amplify upon these particulars.

XV

OF SOME EXCESSES AND EVILS IN THE COMMONWEALTH, WHICH NOTWITHSTANDING DECAY NOT OUR TRADE NOR TREASURE.

XV

OF SOME EXCESSES AND EVILS IN THE COMMONWEALTH, WHICH NOTWITHSTANDING DECAY NOT OUR TRADE NOR TREASURE.

It is not my intent to extenuate or excuse any the least excess or evil in the Commonwealth, but rather highly to commend and approve that which by others hath been spoken and written against such abuses. Yet in this discourse of Treasure, as I have already set down affirmatively, which are the true causes that may either augment or decrease the same: so is it not impertinent to continue my negative declarations of those enormities and actions which cannot work these effects as some men have supposed. For in redress of this important business, if we mistake the nature of the Malady, we shall ever apply such cures as will at least delay, if not confound the Remedy.

Let us then begin with Usury, which if it might be turned into Charity, and that they who are Rich would lend to the poor freely; it were a work pleasing to Almighty God, and profitable to the Commonwealth. But taking it in the degree it now stands; How can we well say, That as Usury encreaseth, so Trade decreaseth? For although it is true that some men give over trading, and buy Lands, or put out their Money to use when they are grown rich, or old, or for some other the like occasions; yet for all this it doth not follow, that the quantity of the trade must lessen; for this course in the rich giveth opportunity presently to the younger & poorer Merchants to rise in the world, and to enlarge their dealings; to the performance whereof, if they want means of their own, they may, and do, take it up at interest: so that our money lies not dead, it is still traded. How many Merchants, and Shopkeepers have begun with little or nothing of their own, and yet are grown very rich by trading with other mens money? do we not know, that when trading is quick and good, many men, by means of their experience, and having credit to take up money at interest, do trade for much more than they are worth of their own stock? by which diligence of the industrious, the affairs of the Commonwealth are increased, the moneys of Widows, Orphans, Lawyers, Gentlemen and others, are employed in the course of Forraign Trade, which themselves have no skill to perform. We find at this present, that notwithstanding the Poverty we are fallen into by the Excesses and

Losses of late times, yet that many men have much money in their chests; and know not how to dispose thereof, because the Merchant will not take the same at interest (although at low rates) in regard there is a stop of trade in Spain and in France, whereby he cannot employ his own meanes, much less other mens moneys. So that for these, and some other reasons which might be alledged, we might conclude, contrary to those who affirm, that Trade decreaseth as Usury encreaseth, for they rise and fall together.

In the next place, we hear our Lawyers much condemned; the vexation and charges by multiplicity of Sutes do exceed all the other Kingdomes of Christendome, but whether this proceed from the Lawyers Covetousness, or the Peoples Perverseness, it is a great question. And let this be as it may, I will enquire no farther therein than our present discourse doth require, concerning the decay of our Trade and impoverishing of the Kingdom: Sure I am, that Sutes in Law make many a man poor and penniless, but how it should make us trade for less by one single penny, I cannot well conceive. For although amongst the great number of them who are vexed and undone by controversies, there be ever some Merchants; yet we know, that one mans necessity becomes another mans opportunity. I never knew as yet, a decay in our Trade and Treasure for want of Merchants or Means to employ us, but rather by excessive Consumption of Forraign Wares at home, or by a declination in the vent of our Commodities abroad, caused either by the ruinous effects of Wars, or some alterations in the times of Peace, whereof I have spoken more fully in the third Chapter. But, to conclude with the Lawyers, I say, that their noble Profession is necessary for all, and their Cases, Quillets, Delayes and Charges, are mischievous to many; these things indeed are Cankers in the Estates of particular men, but not of the Common-wealth, as some suppose, for one mans loss becomes another mans gain, it is still in the Kingdome, I wish it might as surely remain in the right places.

Lastly, all kind of Bounty and Pomp is not to be avoided, for if we should become so frugal, that we would use few or no Forraign wares, how shall we then vent our own commodities? what will become of our Ships, Mariners, Munitions, our poor Artificers, and many others? doe we hope that other Countreys will afford us money for All our wares, without buying or bartering for Some of theirs? this would prove a vain expectation; it is more safe and sure to run a middle course by spending moderately, which will purchase treasure plentifully.

Again, the pomp of Buildings, Apparel, and the like, in the Nobility, Gentry, and other able persons, cannot impoverish the Kingdome; if it be done with curious and costly works upon our Materials, and by our own people, it will maintain the poor with the purse of the rich, which is the best distribution of the Common-wealth. But if any man say, that when the people want work, then the Fishing-trade would be a better employment, and far more profitable; I subscribe willingly. For in that great business there is means enough to employ both rich and poor, whereof there hath been much said and written: it resteth only that something might be as well effected for the honour and wealth, both of the King and his Kingdoms.

XVI

HOW THE REVENUES AND INCOMES OF PRINCES MAY JUSTLY BE RAISED.

XVI

HOW THE REVENUES AND INCOMES OF PRINCES MAY JUSTLY BE RAISED.

Now that we have set down the true course by which a Kingdom may be enriched with treasure; In the next place we will endeavour to shew the ways and means by which a King may justly share therein without the hurt or oppression of his Subjects. The Revenues of Princes as they differ much in quantity, according to the greatness, riches and trade of their respective dominions; so likewise is there great diversity used in procuring the same, according to the constitution of the Countreys, the government, laws and customs of the people, which no Prince can alter but with much difficulty and danger. Some Kings have their Crown Lands, the first fruits upon Ecclesiastical Livings, Customs, Tolls and Imposts upon all trade to and from forraign Countries; Lones, Donations and Subsidies upon all necessary occasions. Other Princes and States leaving the three last, do add unto the rest, a custom upon all new wares transported from one City, to be used in any other City or place of their own dominions, customs upon every alienation or sale of live Cattel, Lands, Houses, and the portions or marriage mony of women, license mony upon all Victualling houses and Inkeepers, head mony, Custom upon all the Corn, Wine, Oyl, Salt and the like, which grow and are consumed in their own dominions, &c. All which seem to be a rabble of oppressions, serving to enrich those Princes which exact them, and to make the people poor and miserable which endure them; especially in those Countreys where these burdens are laid at heavy rates, at 4, 5 ,6, and 7. per cent. But when all the circumstances and distinction of places are duly considered, they will be found not only necessary and therefore lawful to be used in some States, but also in divers respects very profitable to the Commonwealth.

First there are some States, as namely Venice, Florence, Genoua, the united Provinces of the Low Countreys, and others, which are singular for beauty, and excellent both for natural and artificial strength, having likewise rich Subjects: yet being of no very great extent, nor enjoying such wealth by ordinary revenues as might support them against the suddain and powerful invasions of those mighty Princes which do environ them; they are therefore enforced to strengthen themselves not only with confederates and Leagues (which may often fail them in their greatest need) but also by massing up store of treasure and Munition by those extraordinary courses before written, which cannot deceive them, but will ever be ready to make a good defence, and to offend or divert their enemies.

Neither are these heavy Contributions so hurtfull to the happinesse of the people, as they are commonly esteemed: for as the food and rayment of the poor is made dear by Excise, so doth the price of their labour rise in proportion; whereby the burden (if any be) is still upon the rich, who are either idle, or at least work not in this kind, yet have they the use and are the great consumers of the poors labour: Neither do the rich neglect in their several places and callings to advance their endeavours according to those times which do exhaust their means and revenues wherein if they should peradventure fail, and therefore be forced to abate their sinful excess and idle retainers; what is all this but happiness in a Commonwealth, when vertue, plenty and arts shall thus be advanced all together? Nor can it be truly said that a Kingdom is impoverished where the loss of the people is the gain of the King, from whom also such yearly Incomes have their annual issue to the benefit of his Subjects; except only that part of the treasure which is laid up for the publique good; wherein likewise they who suffer have their safety, and therefore such contributions are both just and profitable.

Yet here we must confess, that as the best things may be corrupted, so these taxes may be abused and the Commonwealth notoriously wronged when they are vainly wasted and consumed by a Prince, either upon his own excessive pleasures, or upon unworthy persons, such as deserve neither rewards nor countenance from the Majesty of a Prince: but these dangerous disorders are seldom seen, especially in such States as are aforenamed, because the disposing of the publique treasure is in the power and under the discretion of many; Neither is it unknown to all other Principalities and Governments that the end of such Excesses is ever ruinous, for they cause great want and poverty, which often drives them from all order to exorbitance, and therefore it is common policy amongst Princes to prevent such mischiefs with great care and providence, by doing nothing that may cause the Nobility to despair of their safety, nor leaving any thing undone which may gain the good will of the Commonalty to keep all in due obedience.

Some States cannot subsist, but by the means of heavy taxes.

But now before we end this point in hand, we must remember likewise that all bodies are not of one and the same constitution, for that which is physick to One man, is little better than poyson to another; The States aforewritten, and divers others like to them cannot subsist but by the help of those extraordinary contributions, whereof we have spoken, because they are not able otherwise in short time to raise sufficient treasure to defend themselves against a potent enemy, who hath power to invade them on the suddain, as is already declared. But a mighty Prince whose dominions are great and united, his Subjects many and Loyal, his Countries rich both by nature and traffique, his Victuals and warlike provisions plentiful and ready, his situation easy to offend others, and difficult to be invaded, his harbors good, his Navy strong, his alliance powerfull, and his ordinary revenues sufficient, royally to support the Majesty of his State, besides a reasonable sum which may be advanc'd to lay up yearly in treasure for future occasions: shall not all these blessings (being well ordered) enable a Prince against the suddain invasion of any mighty enemy, without imposing those extraordinary and heavy taxes? shall not the wealthy and loyal subjects of such a great and just Prince maintain his Honour and their own Liberties with life and goods, always supplying the Treasure of their Soveraign, untill by a well ordered War he may inforce a happy Peace? Yes verily, it cannot otherwise be expected. And thus shall a mighty Prince be more powerful in preserving the wealth and love of his Subjects, than by treasuring up their riches with unnecessary taxes, which cannot but alter and provoke them.

Princes, who have no just cause to lay rextraordinary and heavy taxes upon their Subjects.

Yea, but say some men, we may easily contradict all this by example taken from some of the greatest Monarchs of Christendome, who, besides those Incomes which here are termed ordinary, they adde likewise all, or the most of the other heavy Contributions. All which we grant, and more; for they use also to sell their Offices & Places of Justice, which is an act both base & wicked, because it robbeth worthy men of their Merits, & betrayeth the cause of the innocent, whereby God is displeased, the people oppressed, and Vertue banished from such unhappy Kingdomes: Shall we then say, that these things are lawfull and necessary because they are used? God forbid, we know better, and we are well assured that these exactions are not taken for a necessary defence of their own rights, but through pride and covetousness to add Kingdome to Kingdome, and so to usurp the right of others: which actions of Impiety are ever shadowed with some fair pretence of Sanctity, as being done for the Catholick Cause, the propagation of the Church, the suppression of Hereticks, and such like delusions, serving onely to further their own ambition, whereof in this place it shall be needless to make any larger discourse.

The sinister ends which some great Princes have in laying heavy taxes upon their subjects.

XVII

WHETHER IT BE NECESSARY FOR GREAT PRINCES TO LAY UP STORE OF TREASURE.

XVII

WHETHER IT BE NECESSARY FOR GREAT PRINCES TO LAY UP STORE OF TREASURE.

Before we set down the quantity of Treasure which Princes may conveniently lay up yearly without hurting the Common-wealth, it will be fit to examine whether the act it self of Treasuring be necessary: for in common conference we ever find some men who do so much dote or hope upon the Liberality of Princes, that they term it baseness, and conceive it needless for them to lay up store of Treasure, accounting the honour and safety of great Princes to consist more in their Bounty, than in their Money, which they labour to confirm by the examples of Caesar, Alexander, and others, who hating covetousness, atchieved many acts and victories by lavish gifts and liberal expences. Unto which they add also the little fruit which came by that great summ of money which King David laid up and left to his son

Solomon, who notwithstanding this, and all his other rich Presents and wealthy Traffique in a quiet reign, consumed all with pomp and vain delights, excepting only that which was spent in building of the Temple. Whereupon (say they) if so much treasure gathered up by so just a King, effect so little, what shall we hope for by the endeavours of this kind in other Princes? Sardanapalus left ten millions of pounds to them that slew him. Darius left twenty millions of pounds to Alexander that took him; Nero being left rich, and extorting much from his best Subjects, gave away above twelve millions of pounds to his base flatterers and such unworthy persons, which caused Galba after him to revoke those gifts. A Prince who hath store of mony hates peace, despiseth the friendship of his Neighbours and Allies, enters not only into unnecessary, but also into dangerous Wars, to the ruin and over-throw (sometimes) of his own estate: All which, with divers other weak arguments of this kind, (which for brevity I omit) make nothing against the lawful gathering and massing up of Treasure by wise and provident Princes, if they be rightly understood.

For first, concerning those worthies who have obtained to the highest top of honour and dignity, by their great gifts and expences, who knows not that this hath been done rather upon the spoils of their Enemies than out of their own Cofers, which is indeed a Bounty that causeth neither loss nor peril?

Whereas on the contrary, those Princes which do not providently lay up Treasure, or do immoderately consume the same when they have it, will sodainly come to want and misery; for there is nothing doth so soon decay as Excessive Bounty, in using whereof they want the means to use it. And this was King Solomons case, notwithstanding, his infinite Treasure, which made him over-burthen his Subjects in such a manner, that (for this cause) many of them rebelled against his son Rehoboam, who thereby lost a great part of his dominions, being so grosly mis-led by his young Counsellors. Therefore a Prince that will not oppress his people, and yet be able to maintain his Estate, and defend his Right, that will not run himself into Poverty, Contempt, Hate, and Danger, must lay up treasure, and be thrifty, for further proof whereof I might yet produce some other examples, which here I do omit as needless.

Excess and bounty brings beggary, which makes most men devise in their heads how to extort and get mony into their hands.

Only I will add this as a necessary rule to be observed, that when more treasure must be raised than can be received by the ordinary taxes, it ought ever to be done with equality to avoid the hate of the people, who are never pleased except their contributions be granted by general consent: For which purpose the invention of Parliaments is an excellent policie of Government, to keep a sweet concord between a King and his Subjects, by restraining the Insolency of the Nobility, and redressing the Injuries of the

Commons, without engaging a Prince to adhere to either party, but indifferently to favour both. There could nothing be devised with more judgment for the common quiet of a Kingdom, or with greater care for the safety of a King, who hereby hath also good means to dispatch those things by others, which will move envy, and to execute that himself which will merit thanks.

XVIII

HOW MUCH TREASURE A PRINCE MAY CONVENIENTLY LAY UP YEARLY.

XVIII

HOW MUCH TREASURE A PRINCE MAY CONVENIENTLY LAY UP YEARLY.

Thus far we have shewed the ordinary and extraordinary incomes of Princes, the conveniency thereof, and to whom only it doth necessarily and justly belong, to take the extraordinary contributions of their Subjects. It resteth now to examine what proportion of treasure each particular Prince may conveniently lay up yearly. This business doth seem at the first very plain and easy, for if a Prince have two millions yearly revenue, and spend but one, why should he not lay up the other? Indeed I must confess that this course is ordinary in the means and gettings of private men, but in the affairs of Princes it is far different, there are other circumstances to be considered; for although the revenue of a King should be very great, yet if the gain of the Kingdom be but small, this latter must ever give rule and proportion to that Treasure

Forraign Trade must give proportion to a Princes treasure which is laid up yearly.

which may conveniently be laid up yearly, for if he should mass up more mony than is gained by the over-balance of his forraign trade, he shall not Fleece, but Flea his Subjects, and so with their ruin overthrow himself for want of future sheerings. To make this plain, suppose a Kingdom to be so rich by nature and art, that it may supply it self of forraign wares by trade, and yet advance yearly 200000 l. in ready mony: Next suppose all the Kings revenues to be 900000 l. and his expences but 400000 l. whereby he may lay up 300000 l. more in his Coffers yearly than the whole Kingdoms gain from strangers by forraign trade; who sees not then that all the mony in such a State, would suddenly be drawn into the Princes treasure, whereby the life of lands and arts must fail and fall to the ruin both of the publick and private wealth? So that a King who desires to lay up much mony must endeavour by all good means to maintain and encrease his forraign trade, because it is the sole way not only to lead him to his own ends, but also to enrich his Subjects to his farther benefit: for a Prince is esteemed no less powerful by having many rich and well affected Subjects, than by possessing much treasure in his Coffers.

A Prince whose Subjects have but little forraign Trade cannot lay up much money

But here we must meet with an Objection, which peradventure may be made concerning such States (whereof I have formerly spoken) which are of no great extent, and yet bordering upon mighty Princes, are therefore constrained to lay extraordinary taxes upon their subjects, whereby they procure to themselves very great incomes yearly, and are richly provided against any Forraign Invasions; yet have they no such great trade with Strangers, as that the over-balance or gain of the same may suffice to lay up the one half of that which they advance yearly, besides their own expences.

To this the answer is, that stil the gain of their Forraign Trade must be the rule of laying up their treasure, the which although it should not be much yearly, yet in the time of a long continued peace, and being well managed to advantage, it will become a great summe of money, able to make a long defence, which may end or divert the war. Neither are all the advances of Princes strictly tied to be massed up in treasure, for they have other no less necessary and profitable wayes to make them rich and powerfull, by issuing out continually a great part of the mony of their yearly Incomes to their Subjects from whom it was first taken; as namely, by employing them to make Ships of War, with all the provisions thereunto belonging, to build and repair Forts, to buy and store up Corn in the Granaries of each Province for a years use (at least) aforehand, to serve in occasion of Dearth, which cannot be neglected by a State but with great danger, to erect Banks with their money for the encrease of their subjects trade, to maintain in their pay, Collonels, Captains, Souldiers, Commanders, Mariners,

Munition for war ought to be kept in divers places of the State, to prevent the loss of all by trechery in one place.

and others, both by Sea and Land, with good discipline, to fill their Store-houses (in sundry strong places) and to abound in Gunpowder, Brimstone, Saltpeter, Shot, Ordnance, Musquets, Swords, Pikes, Armours, Horses, and in many other such like Provisions fitting War; all which will make them to be feared abroad, and loved at home, especially if care be taken that all (as neer as possible) be made out of the Matter and Manufacture of their own subjects, which bear the burden of the yearly Contributions; for a Prince (in this case) is like the stomach in the body, which if it cease to digest and distribute to the other members, it doth no sooner corrupt them, but it destroyes it self.

Thus we have seen that a small State may lay up a great wealth in necessary provisions, which are Princes Jewels, no less precious than their Treasure, for in time of need they are ready, and cannot otherwise be had (in some places) on the suddain, whereby a State may be lost, whilest Munition is in providing: so that we may account that Prince as poor who can have no wares to buy at his need, as he that hath no money to buy wares; for although Treasure is said to be the sinews of the War, yet this is so because it doth provide, unite and move the power of men, victuals, and munition where and when the cause doth require; but if these things be wanting in due time, what shall we then do with our mony? the consideration of this, doth cause divers well-governed States to be exceeding provident and well furnished of such provisions, especially those Granaries and Storehouses with that famous Arsenal of the Venetians, are to be admired for the magnificence of the buildings, the quantity of the Munitions and Stores both for Sea and Land, the multitude of the workmen, the diversity and excellency of the Arts, with the order of the government. They are rare and worthy things for Princes to behold and imitate; for Majesty without providence of competent force, and ability of necessary provisions is unassured.

XIX

OF SOME DIFFERENT EFFECTS, WHICH PROCEED FROM NATURALL AND ARTIFICIAL WEALTH.

XIX

OF SOME DIFFERENT EFFECTS, WHICH PROCEED FROM NATURALL AND ARTIFICIAL WEALTH.

In the latter end of the third Chapter of this Book, I have already written something concerning Natural and Artificial Wealth, and therein shewed how much Art doth add to Nature; but it is yet needful to handle these particulars apart, that so we may the better discern their severall operations in a Common-wealth. For the effecting whereof, I might draw some comparisons from Turkey and Italy, or from some other remote Countreys, but I will not range so far, having matter sufficient here in Great Britain and the united Provinces of the Low Countreys, to make this business plain: wherefore, in the first place, we will begin with England briefly, and onely in general terms, to shew the natural riches of this famous Nation, with some principal effects which they produce in the disposition of the people, and strength of the Kingdome.

If we duly consider Englands Largeness, Beauty, Fertility, Strength, both by Sea and Land, in multitude of warlike People, Horses, Ships, Ammunition, advantageous situation for Defence and Trade, number of Sea-ports and Harbours, which are of difficult access to Enemies, and of easie out-let to the Inhabitants wealth by excellent Fleece-wools, Iron, Lead, Tynn, Saffron, Corn, Victuals, Hides, Wax, and other natural Endowments; we shall find this Kingdome capable to sit as master of a Monarchy. For what greater glory and advantage can any powerful Nation have, than to be thus richly and naturally possessed of all things needful for Food, Rayment, War, and Peace, not onely for its own plentiful use, but also to supply the wants of other Nations, in such a measure, that much money may be thereby gotten yearly, to make the happiness compleat. For experience telleth us, that notwithstanding that excessive Consumption of this Kingdome alone, to say nothing of Scotland, there is exported communibus annis of our own native commodities for the value of twenty two hundred thousand pounds Sterling, or somewhat more; so that if we were not too much affected to Pride, monstrous Fashions, and Riot, above all other Nations, one million and an half of pounds might plentifully supply our unnecessary wants (as I may term them) of Silks, Sugars, Spices, Fruits, and all others; so that seven hundred thousand pounds might be yearly treasur'd up in money to make the Kingdome exceeding rich and powerful in short time. But this great plenty which we enjoy, makes us a people not only vicious and excessive, wasteful of the means we have, but also improvident & careless of much other wealth that shamefully we lose, which is, the Fishing in his Majesty's Seas of England, Scotland, and Ireland, being of no less consequence than all our other riches which we export and vent to Strangers, whilest in the mean time (through lewd idleness) great multitudes of our people cheat, roar, rob, hang, beg, cant, pine and perish, which by this means and maintenance might be much encreased, to the further wealth and strength of these Kingdomes, especially by Sea, for our own safety, and terrour of our enemies. The endeavours of the industrious Dutch do give sufficient testimony of this truth, to our great shame, and no less perill, if it have not a timely prevention: for, whilest we leave our wonted honourable exercises and studies, following our pleasures, and of late years besotting our selves with pipe and pot, in a beastly manner, sucking smoak, and drinking healths, until death stares many in the face; the said Dutch have well-neer left this swinish vice, and taken up our wonted valour, which we have often so well performed both by Sea and Land, and particularly in their defence, although they are not now so thankful as to acknowledge the same. The

The fruits of Idleness, which are Englands common reproches among Strangers.

The Netherlanders ingratitude.

summm of all is this, that the general leprosie of our Piping, Potting, Feasting, Fashions, and mis-spending of our time in Idleness and Pleasure (contrary to the Law of God, and the use of other Nations) hath made us effeminate in our bodies, weak in our knowledg, poor in our Treasure, declined in our Valour, unfortunate in our Enterprises, and contemned by our Enemies. I write the more of these excesses, because they do so greatly waste our wealth, which is the main subject of this whole Books discourse: and indeed our wealth might be a rare discourse for all Christendome to admire and fear, if we would but add Art to Nature, our labour to our natural means; the neglect whereof hath given a notable advantage to other nations, & especially to the Hollanders, whereof I will briefly say something in the next place.

But first, I will deliver my opinion concerning our Clothing, which although it is the greatest Wealth and best Employment of the Poor of this Kingdome, yet nevertheless we may peradventure employ our selves with better Plenty, Safety, and Profit in using more Tillage and Fishing, than to trust so wholly to the making of Cloth; for in times of War, or by other occasions, if some forraign Prince should prohibit the use thereof in their dominions, it might suddenly cause much poverty and dangerous uproars, especially by our poor people, when they should be deprived of their ordinary maintenance, which cannot so easily fail them when their labours should be divided into the said diversity of employments; whereby also many thousands would be the better enabled to do the Kingdom good service in occasion of war, especially by Sea: And so leaving England, wee will pass over into the United Provinces of the Netherlands.

As plenty and power doe make a nation vicious and improvident, so penury and want doe make a people wise and industrious: concerning the last of these I might instance divers Commonwealths of Christendom, who having little or nothing in their own Territories, do notwithstanding purchase great wealth and strength by their industrious commerce with strangers, amongst which the united Provinces of the Low Countreys are now of greatest note and fame: For since they have cast off the yoke of Spanish slavery, how wonderfully are they improved in all humane policy? What great means have they obtained to defend their liberty against the power of so great an Enemy? and is not all this performed by their continual industry in the trade of Merchandize? are not their Provinces the Magazines and Store-houses of wares for most places of Christendom, whereby their Wealth, Shipping, Mariners, Arts, People, and thereby the publique Revenues and Excizes are grown to a wonderful height? If we compare the times of their subjection, to their present estate, they seem not the same people; for

The Hollanders improvement and industry.

Those Princes which do willingly support the Dutch, would as resolutely resist the Spaniard.

who knows not that the condition of those Provinces was mean and turbulent under the Spaniards government, which brought rather a greater charge than a further strength to their ambition; neither would it prove over difficult for the neighbour Princes in short time to reduce those Countreys to their former estate again, if their own safety did require the same, as certainly it would if the Spaniard were sole Lord of those Netherlands; but our discourse tends not to shew the means of those mutations, otherwise than to find out the chief foundation of the Hollanders wealth and greatness: for it seems a wonder to the world, that such a small Countrey, not fully so big as two of our best Shires, having little natural Wealth, Victuals, Timber, or other necessary amunitions, either for war or peace, should notwithstanding possess them all in such extraordinary plenty, that besides their own wants (which are very great) they can and do likewise serve and sell to other Princes, Ships, Ordnance, Cordage, Corn, Powder, Shot, and what not, which by their industrious trading they gather from all the quarters of the world: In which courses they are not less injurious to supplant others (especially the English) than they are careful to strengthen themselves. And to effect this and more than hath been said (which is their war with Spain) they have little foundation besides the Fishing, which is permitted them in His Majesties Seas, being indeed the means of an incredible wealth and

Much Policy, but little Honesty.

strength, both by Sea and Land, as Robert Hichcock, Tobias Gentleman, and others have published at large in print to them that list to read. And the States General themselves in their proclamation have ingeniously set out the worth thereof in these words following, *The great Fishing and catching of Herrings is the cheifest trade and principal Gold Mine of the United Provinces, whereby many thousands of Housholds, Families, Handicrafts, Trades and Occupations are set on work, well maintained and prosper, especially the sailing and navigation, as well within as without these Countreys is kept in great estimation; Moreover many returns of mony, with the encrease of the means, Convoys, Customs and revenues of these Countreys are augmented thereby and prosper,* with other words following, as is at large expressed in the said Proclamations, set forth by the States General for the preservation of the said trade of Fishing; without which it is apparent that they cannot long subsist in Soveraignty; for if this foundation perish, the whole building of their wealth and strength both by Sea and Land must fall; for the multitude of their Shipping would suddainly decay, their revenues and customs would become small, their Countreys would be depopulated for want of maintenance, whereby the Excise must fail, and all their other trades to the East Indies or elsewhere must faint. So that the glory and power of these Netherlanders consisteth in this fishing of Herrings, Ling

Part of the States Proclamation, dated in the Hague, 19. July 1624.

and Cod in His Majesties Seas. It resteth therefore to know what right or title they have thereunto, and how they are able to possess and keep the same against all other Nations.

The answers to these two questions are not difficult: for first, it is not the Netherlandish Author of Mare Liberum, that can entitle them to Fish in His Majesties Seas. For besides the Justice of the cause, and examples of other Countreys, which might be alleged, I will only say, that such titles would be sooner decided by swords, than with words; I do beleeve indeed that it is free for the Fish to come thither at their pleasure, but for the Dutch to catch and carry them away from thence without His Majesties licence, I harbour no such thought. There may be good policy to connive still, and so long to permit them this fishing as they are in perfect league with England, and in war with Spain. But if the Spaniards were Masters of the United Provinces as heretofore, it would neerly concern these Kingdoms to claim their own right, and carefully to make as good use thereof for increase of their wealth and strength, to oppose that potent enemy, as now the Netherlanders do, and are thereby well enabled for the same purpose: by which particular alone they are ever bound to acknowledge their strong alliance with England, above all other Nations, for there is none that hath the like good means to lend them such a powerful maintenance. Nor were it possible for the

Money and Fishing compared.

Spaniard (if he had those Countreys again) to make a new Foundation with the power of his money, to encrease his strength, either by Sea or Land, to offend these Kingdoms, more than he is now able to perform with the conveniency of those Provinces which he hath already in his possession; for it is not the Place, but the Employment, not the barren Netherlands, but the rich Fishing, which gives Foundation, Trade, and Subsistence to those multitudes of Ships, Arts and People, whereby also the Excises and other publick Revenues are continued, and without which Employment all the said great Dependences must necessarily disbandon and fail in very short time. For although I confess, that store of money may bring them materials (which they altogether want) and Artsmen to build them Shipping, yet where are the wares to fraight and maintain them? if money then shall be the onely means to send them out in Trade, what a poor number of Ships will this employ? or if the uncertain occasions of War must support them, will not this require another Indies, and all too little to maintain the tenth part of so many Ships and Men as the Hollanders do now set on work by the Fishing and other Trades thereon depending? But if it be yet said, that the Spaniard being Lord of all those Netherlands, his expence of the present War there will cease, and so this power may be turned upon us. The answer is, that when Princes send great Forces abroad to invade others, they must likewise encrease their charge and strength at home, to defend themselves; and also we must consider, that if the Spaniard will attempt any thing upon these Kingdomes, he must consume a great part of his Treasure in Shipping, whereby the means of his invading power of Money and Men to land will be much less than now it is in the Low Countreys: Nor should we regard them, but be ever ready to beard them, when our Wealth and Strength by Sea and Land might be so much encreased by the possession and practise of our Fishing, of which particular I will yet say something more when occasion shall be offered in that which followeth. And here in this place I will onely add, that if the Spaniard were sole Lord of all the Netherlands, he must then necessarily drive a great trade by Sea, to supply the common wants of those Countreys, whereby in occasion of war, we should have means daily to take much wealth from him; whereas now the Spaniard using little or no trade in these Seas, but imploying his Ships of warre to the uttermost of his power, he only takes, and we lose great matters continually.

Now concerning the second question, Whether the Hollanders be able to possess and keep this fishing against all other Nations. It is very probable, that although they claim now no other right than their own freedome in this Fishing, seeming to leave the like to all others; yet if the practise of any Nation should seek either to Fish with them or to supplant them, they would be both ready and able to defend this Golden Mine, against the strongest opposition except England, whose harbours and In-lands with other daily reliefs are very needful, if not absolutely necessary for this employment, and whose Power also by Sea, is able (in short time) to give this business disturbance, and utter ruin, if the occasion should be so urgent as is afore supposed: Neither is it enough for any man to contradict all this by saying the Hollanders are very strong by Sea, when both Sea and Land encounter them with a greater power: we must observe from whence their strength doth grow, and if the root may once be spoiled, the branches soon will wither; and therefore it were an error to esteem, or value them according to the present power and wealth, which they have obtained by trade or purchase; for although this were far greater than indeed it is, yet would it soon be consumed in a chargeable war against a potent enemy, when the current of those Accidents may be stopt and turned by preventing the substance it self (which is the Fishing in His Majesties Seas) that gives Foundation, and is the very Foundation of their strength and happiness: The United Provinces (we know) are like a fair bird suited with goodly borrowed plumes; but if every Fowl should take his feather, this bird would rest neer naked; Nor have we ever seen these Netherlanders as yet in their greatest occasions to set forth neer so many ships of war as the English have often done without any hindrance of their ordinary traffique; It is true indeed, they have an infinite number of weak Ships to fish with, and fetch Corn, Salt, &c. for their own victualling and trading, the like to fetch Timber, Plank, Boords, Pitch, Hemp, Tar, Flax, Masts, Cordage, and other Ammunitions to make those multitudes of Ships, which unto them are as our Ploughs to us, the which except they stir, the people starve; their Shipping therefore cannot be spared from their traffique (as ours may if occasion require) no not for a very short time, without utter ruin, because it is the daily maintenance of their great multitudes which gain their living but from hand to mouths upon which also depends the great excises, and other publique revenues, which support the State it self: Neither indeed are those Vessels strong or fit for war; and in their proper use of Fishing and trade they would become the riches, or the purchase of a potent Enemy by Sea, as they partly find by one poor town of Dunkirk, notwithstanding their great charge of Men of war, strong Convoys, and other commendable diligence, which continually they use to prevent this mischief: but if the occasion of a more powerful enemy by Sea should force them to double or treble those charges, we may well doubt the means of their continuance, especially when (by us) their fishing might nevertheless be prevented,

The Netherlanders Ploughs.

Men who speak by affection or tradition, not from reason.

which should procure the maintenance. These and other circumstances make me often wonder, when I hear the Dutch vain-gloriously to brag, and many English simply to believe, that the United Provinces are our Forts, Bulwarks, Walls, out-works, and I know not what, without which we cannot long subsist against the Spanish forces; when in truth, we are the main fountain of their happiness, both for war and peace; for trade and treasure, for Munition and Men, spending our bloud in their defence; whilst their people are preserved to conquer in the Indies, and to reap the fruits of a rich traffique out of our own bosoms; which being assumed to our selves (as we have right and power to do) would mightily encrease the breed of our people by this good means of their maintenance, and well enable us against the strongest enemy, and force likewise great multitudes of those Netherlanders themselves to seek their living here with us for want of better maintenance: whereby our many decayed Sea-towns and Castles would soon be re-edified and populated in more ample manner than formerly they were in their best estate. And thus these forces being united, would be ever more ready, sure, and vigorous than a great strength that lies divided, which is always subject to delays, diversion, and other jealousies, of all which we ought not to be ignorant, but perfectly to know, and use our own strength when we have occasion,

The Hollanders main supportance is Englands good Alliance.

and especially we must ever be watchful to preserve this strength, lest the subtilty of the Dutch (under some fair shews and with their mony) prevail, as peradventure they lately practised in Scotland, to have had a Patent for the possessing, inhabiting, and fortifying of that excellent Island of Lewis in the Orcades; whose scituation, harbours, fishing, fertility, largeness and other advantages, would have made them able (in short time) to offend these Kingdoms by suddain invasions, and to have defended the aforesaid Fishing against his Majesties greatest power, and also to send out and return home their Shipping prosperously that way, to and from the East and West Indies, Spain, the Straights, and other places, without passing through his Majesty's narrow Seas, where in all occasions this Kingdome now hath so great advantage to take their Ships, and prevent their best Trades, which would soon bring them to ruine, whereby (as they well know) we have a greater tie and power over them than any other Nation. And howsoever the said Island of Lewis might have been obtained in the name of private men, and under the fair pretence of bringing Commerce into those remote parts of Scotland; yet in the end, when the work had been brought to any good perfection, the possession and power would no doubt have come to the Lords, the States General, even as we know they have lately gotten divers places of great Strength and Wealth in the East Indies, in the names and with the purse of their Merchants, whereby also their actions herein have been obscured & made less notorious unto the world, untill they had obtain'd their ends, which are of such consequence, that it doth much concern this Nation in particular, carefully to observe their proceedings, for they notoriously follow the steps of that valiant and politick Captain, Philip of Macedon, whose Maxim was, That where force could not prevail, he alwayes used bribes, and money to corrupt those who might advance his fortune; by which policy he gave foundation to a Monarchy; & what know we but that the Dutch may aim at some such Soveraignty, when they shall find their Indian attempts and other subtil plots succeed so prosperously? Do we not see their Lands are now become too little to contain this swelling people, whereby their Ships and Seas are made the Habitations of great multitudes? and yet, to give them further breed, are they not spared from their own wars to enrich the State and themselves by Trade and Arts? whilest by this policy many thousands of strangers are also drawn thither for performance of their martial employments, whereby the great revenue of their Excises is so much the more encreased, and all things so subtilly contrived, that although the forraign Souldier be well paid, yet all must be there again expended; and thus the Wealth remains still in their own Countreys; nor are the strangers enriched which do them this great service.

Where force fails, yet money prevails; thus hopes the Hollanders.

I have heard some Italians wisely and worthily discourse of the natural Strength and Wealth of England, which they make to be matchless, if we should (but in part) apply our selves to such policies and endeavours as are very commonly used in some other Countreys of Europe; and much they have admired, that our thoughts and jealousies attend only upon the Spanish and French greatness, never once suspecting, but constantly embracing the Netherlanders as our best Friends and Allies; when in truth (as they well observe) there are no people in Christendome who do more undermine, hurt, and eclipse us daily in our Navigation and Trades, both abroad and at home; and this not only in the rich Fishing in his Majesty's Seas (whereof we have already written) but also in our Inland trades between City and City, in the Manufactures of Silk, Woolls, and the like, made here in this Kingdom, wherein they never give employment or education in their Arts to the English, but ever (according to the custome of the Jewes, where they abide in Turkey, and divers places of Christendome) they live wholly to themselves in their own Tribes. So that we may truly say of the Dutch, that although they are amongst us, yet certainly they are not of us, no not they who are born and bred here in our own Countrey, for stil they will be Dutch, not having so much as one drop of English bloud in their hearts.

More might be written of these

Netherlanders pride and ambitious endeavours, whereby they hope in time to grow mighty, if they be not prevented, and much more may be said of their cruel and unjust violence used (especially to their best friends, the English) in matters of bloud, trade, and other profits, where they have had advantage and power to perform it: but these things are already published in print to the view and admiration of the world; wherefore I will conclude, and the summ of all is this, that the United Provinces, which now are so great a trouble, if not a terrour to the Spaniard, were heretofore little better than a charge to them in their possession, and would be so again in the like occasion, the reasons whereof I might yet further enlarge; but they are not pertinent to this discourse, more than is already declared, to shew the different effects between Natural and Artificial Wealth: The first of which, as it is most noble and advantagious, being alwayes ready and certain, so doth it make the people careless, proud, and given to all excesses; whereas the second enforceth Vigilancy, Literature, Arts and Policy. My wishes therefore are, that as England doth plentifully enjoy the one, and is fully capable of the other, that our endeavours might as worthily conjoin them both together, to the reformation of our vicious idleness, and greater glory of these famous Kingdomes.

XX

THE ORDER AND MEANS WHEREBY WE MAY DRAW UP THE BALLANCE OF OUR FORRAIGN TRADE.

XX

THE ORDER AND MEANS WHEREBY WE MAY DRAW UP THE BALLANCE OF OUR FORRAIGN TRADE.

Now, that we have sufficiently proved the Ballance of our Forraign Trade to be the true rule of our Treasure; It resteth that we shew by whom and in what manner the said ballance may be drawn up at all times, when it shall please the State to discover how we prosper or decline in this great and weighty business, wherein the Officers of his Majesties Customes are the onely Agents to be employed, because they have the accounts of all the wares which are issued out or brought into the Kingdome; and although (it is true) they cannot exactly set down the cost and charges of other men's goods bought here or beyond the seas; yet nevertheless, if they ground themselves upon the book of Rates, they shall be able to make such an estimate as may well satisfie this enquiry: for it is not expected that such an account can possibly be drawn up to a just ballance, it will suffice onely that the difference be not over great.

How we must value our Exportations and Importations.

First therefore, concerning our Exportations, when we have valued their first cost, we must add twenty-five per cent. thereunto for the charges here, for fraight of Ships, ensurance of the Adventure, and the Merchants Gains; and for our Fishing Trades, which pay no Custome to his Majesty, the value of such Exportations may be easily esteem'd by good observations which have been made, and may continually be made, according to the increase or decrease of those affairs, the present state of this commodity being valued at one hundred and forty thousand pounds issued yearly. Also we must add to our Exportations all the moneys which are carried out in Trade by license from his Majesty.

Secondly, for our Importations of Forraign Wares, the Custome-books serve onely to direct us concerning the quantity, for we must not value them as they are rated here, but as they cost us with all charges laden into our Ships beyond the Seas, in the respective places where they are bought: for the Merchants gain, the charges of Insurance, Fraight of Ships, Customes, Imposts, and other Duties here, which doe greatly indear them unto our use and consumption, are notwithstanding but Commutations amongst our selves, for the Stranger hath no part thereof: wherefore our said Importations ought to be valued at twenty five per cent. less than they are rated to be worth here. And although this may seem to be too great allowance upon many rich Commodities, which come but from the Low Countreys and other places neer hand, yet will it be found reasonable, when we consider it in gross Commodities, and upon Wares laden in remote Countreys, as our Pepper, which cost us, with charges, but four pence the pound in the East Indies, and it is here rated at twenty pence the pound: so that when all is brought into a medium, the valuation ought to be made as afore-written. And therefore, the order which hath been used to multiply the full rates upon wares inwards by twenty, would produce a very great errour in the Ballance, for in this manner the ten thousand bags of Pepper, which this year we have brought hither from the East Indies, should be valued at very near two hundred and fifty thousand pounds, whereas all this Pepper in the Kingdomes accompt, cost not above fifty thousand pounds, because the Indians have had no more of us, although we paid them extraordinary dear prices for the same. All the other charges (as I have said before) is but a change of effects amongst our selves, and from the Subject to the King, which cannot impoverish the Common-wealth. But it is true, that whereas nine thousand bags of the said Pepper are already shipped out for divers forraign parts; These and all other Wares, forraign or domestick, which are thus

The Trade to the East Indies is not onely great in it self, but it doth also make our other trades much greater than they were.

transported Outwards, ought to be cast up by the rates of his Majesties Custome-money, multiplyed by twenty, or rather by twenty five (as I conceive) which will come neerer the reckoning, when we consider all our Trades to bring them into a medium.

Thirdly, we must remember, that all Wares exported or imported by Strangers (in their shipping) be esteemed by themselves, for what they carry out, the Kingdom hath only the first cost and the custom: And what they bring in, we must rate it as it is worth here, the Custom, Impost, and petty charges only deducted.

Lastly, there must be good notice taken of all the great losses which we receive at Sea in our Shipping either outward or homeward bound: for the value of the one is to be deducted from our Exportations, and the value of the other is to be added to our Importations: for to lose and to consume doth produce one and the same reckoning. Likewise if it happen that His Majesty doth make over any great sums of mony by Exchange to maintain a forraign war, where we do not feed and clothe the Souldiers, and Provide the armies, we must deduct all this charge out of our Exportations or add it to our Importations; for this expence doth either carry out or hinder the coming in of so much Treasure. And here we must remember the great collections of mony which are supposed to be made throughout the Realm yearly from our Recusants by Priests and Jesuits, who secretly convey the same unto their Colleges, Cloysters and Nunneries beyond the Seas, from whence it never returns to us again in any kind; therefore if this mischief cannot be prevented, yet it must be esteemed and set down as a cleer loss to the Kingdome, except (to ballance this) we will imagine that as great a value may perhaps come in from forraign Princes to their Pensioners here for Favours or Intelligence, which some States account good Policy, to purchase with great Liberality; the receipt whereof notwithstanding is plain Treachery.

Two Contraries which are both pernicious.

There are yet some other petty things which seem to have reference to this Ballance, of which the said Officers of His Majesties Customs can take no notice, to bring them into the accompt. As namely, the expences of travailers, the gifts to Ambassadors and Strangers, the fraud of some rich goods not entred into the Custom-house, the gain which is made here by Strangers by change and re-change, Interest of mony, ensurance upon English mens goods and their lives: which can be little when the charges of their living here is deducted; besides that the very like advantages are as amply ministred unto the English in forraign Countreys, which doth counterpoize all these things, and therefore they are not considerable in the drawing up of the said Ballance.

XXI

THE CONCLUSION UPON ALL THAT HATH BEEN SAID, CONCERNING THE EXPORTATION OR IMPORTATION OF TREASURE.

XXI

THE CONCLUSION UPON ALL THAT HATH BEEN SAID, CONCERNING THE EXPORTATION OR IMPORTATION OF TREASURE.

The sum of all that hath been spoken, concerning the enriching of the Kingdom, and th' encrease of our treasure by commerce with strangers, is briefly thus. That it is a certain rule in our forraign trade, in those places where our commodities exported are overballanced in value by forraign wares brought into this Realm, there our mony is undervalued in exchange; and where the contrary of this is performed, there our mony is overvalued. But let the Merchants exchange be at a high rate, or at a low rate, or at the Par pro pari, or put down altogether; Let Forraign Princes enhance their Coins, or debase their Standards, and let His Majesty do the like, or keep them constant as they now stand; Let forraign Coins pass current here in all payments at higher rates than they are worth at the Mint; Let the Statutes for employments by Strangers stand in force or be repealed; Let the meer Exchanger do his worst; Let Princes oppress, Lawyers extort, Usurers bite, Prodigals wast, and lastly let Merchants carry out what mony they shall have occasion to use in traffique. Yet all these actions can work no other effects in the course of trade than is declared in this discourse. For so much Treasure only will be brought in or carried out of a Commonwealth, as the Forraign Trade doth over or under ballance in value. And this must come to pass by a Necessity beyond all resistance. So that all other courses (which tend not to this end) howsoever they may seem to force mony into a Kingdom for a time, yet are they (in the end) not only fruitless but also hurtful: they are like to violent flouds which bear down their banks, and suddenly remain dry again for want of waters. Behold then the true form and worth of forraign Trade, which is, The great Revenue of the King, The honour of the Kingdom, The Noble profession of the Merchant, The School of our Arts, The supply of our wants, The employment of our poor, The improvement of our Lands, The Nurcery of our Mariners, The walls of the Kingdoms, The means of our Treasure, The Sinnews of our wars, The terror of our Enemies. For all which great and weighty reasons, do so many well governed States highly countenance the profession, and carefully cherish the action, not only with Policy to encrease it, but also with power to protect it from all forraign injuries: because they know it is a Principal in Reason of State to maintain and defend that which doth Support them and their estates.

FINIS

ALSO AVAILABLE FROM NEWTON PAGE

ALSO AVAILABLE FROM NEWTON PAGE

John Law of Lauriston

Financier and Statesman, Founder of the Bank of France, Originator of the Mississippi Scheme

A. W. Wiston-Glynn

ISBN-13: 978-1934619032

The true story of a Scottish murderer, philanderer, gambler and abscondee who escaped his condemned cell in London to become the darling of the French economy, John Law of Lauriston is an account of the euphoria and wealth Law created by engineering the first stock market boom, and the despair, poverty and destruction which followed its inevitable crash.

ALSO AVAILABLE FROM NEWTON PAGE

The Mississippi Bubble

A Memoir of John Law

Adolphe Thiers

ISBN-13: 978-1934619056

An established classic and authoritative historical analysis of the spectacular rise and fall of the most enigmatic genius in financial and economic history. It provides a compelling biographical narrative of John Law's life, a considered examination of his Mississippi Scheme, and enlightening accounts of both the Darien Expedition and South Sea Bubble.

ALSO AVAILABLE FROM NEWTON PAGE

The Life of John Law

Including a Detailed Account of the Rise, Progress and Termination of the Mississippi System

John Phillip Wood

ISBN-13: 978-1934619018

One of the most cited biographies of John Law in existence. It is both a concise and gripping retelling of the extraordinary life story of the 'first millionaire' and also a very readable and entertaining account of the remarkably swift rise and even swifter decline of both of his influential innovations: the Mississippi Company and the Mississippi Scheme.

ALSO AVAILABLE FROM NEWTON PAGE

The Financier Law

His Scheme and Times: A Graphic Description of the Origin, Maturity and Wreck of the Mississippi Scheme

André Cochut

ISBN-13: 978-1934619049

A richly contextual narrative of the life of John Law, a charismatic Scottish economist and murderer and who would escape execution and use his seemingly effortless financial genius to rise from obscurity to become the most powerful member of the French court, the controller of the French economy, and the richest man the modern world had ever seen.

ALSO AVAILABLE FROM NEWTON PAGE

Letters to John Law

A Letter to Mr. Law
The Case of Mr. Law Truly Stated
A Second Letter to Mr. Law

Selected and introduced by

Gavin John Adams

ISBN-13: 978-1-934619087

This collection of three uncompromising early eighteenth-century propagandist pamphlets documents the wildly contrasting reactions to Law's surprise return to Britain. Crafted by the most prominent journalists, commentators and political agitators of the day, each provides an invaluable contemporaneous social, political and historical record of the most remarkable story in financial history.

ALSO AVAILABLE FROM NEWTON PAGE

Daniel Defoe on John Law and the Mississippi Scheme

The Chimera
The Case of Mr. Law Truly Stated
Selected Journalism 1719-1722

Selected and introduced by

Gavin John Adams

ISBN-13: 978-1934619100

This collection includes: *The Chimera*, a prophetic critique and damnation of John Law's Mississippi Scheme; *The Case of Mr. Law Truly Stated*, a propagandist attack upon Law's return to Britain after the collapse of the Mississippi Scheme and his expulsion from France; and *Selected Journalism* spanning 1719-1722, cataloging Defoe's contemporaneous coverage of the rise and fall of John Law.

ALSO AVAILABLE FROM NEWTON PAGE

John Law's Money and Trade Considered

A Hidden Foundation of
Modern Economic Thought

Edited and introduced by

Gavin John Adams

ISBN-13: 978-1934619094

One of the most influential tracts in economic and financial history. Written in 1705 to prompt political change in Scotland, it includes proposals for new systems of banking and paper money. A pioneering work of staggering originality, it revealed several of the most significant economic concepts ever devised; concepts which would be used without acknowledgement by economists such as Adam Smith and John Maynard Keynes.

53230315R00177

Made in the USA
Middletown, DE
11 July 2019